"Leighann is a seasoned warrior in the fight against the forces of darkness. She's also a gifted communicator. That combination makes this a powerful book. It's full of biblical insight and provides practical applications you will use in every season of your children's lives."

—Dr. Joe Beam, author, *Seeing the Unseen: Preparing Yourself for Spiritual Warfare*

"Leighann McCoy is one of those writers who combine solid scriptural insight and practical truths worked out in the crucible of real-life experience. She opens her life to us, exposing her lived-out pain and struggle with no candy coating. But she lets God tell His story through her story. And she offers His hope and His assurance of victory."

—Jennifer Kennedy Dean, author, *Live a Praying Life*

"This is a life-changing book, whether you are a new or battle-focused warrior! It has clear, biblical, spiritual truths that are critical. God will reveal areas of urgent need for your family. It is a tool to read, highlight, and go back to time and time again."

—Teri Froman, executive director, Pharaoh's Daughters

"*Spiritual Warfare for Your Family* is a game-changer. With a solid scriptural foundation and depth of insight and personal experience, Leighann gives us the tools we need to do battle for our families. She writes as if our lives depend on it, and I believe they do."

—Kaye Hurta, crisis counselor

"I heartily recommend *Spiritual Warfare for Your Family*. From its overall message of victory in Jesus to addressing specific life battles, it will help believers fight. I have witnessed Leighann McCoy's great faith in our great God. Readers will be grateful she chose to share her battlefield knowledge and wisdom."

—Lisa Parnell

Books by Leighann McCoy
from Bethany House Publishers

Spiritual Warfare for Your Family
Spiritual Warfare for Women
A Woman's Guide to Hearing God's Voice

SPIRITUAL WARFARE

for Your
Family

WHAT YOU NEED TO KNOW
TO PROTECT YOUR CHILDREN

Leighann McCoy

BETHANYHOUSE
a division of Baker Publishing Group
Minneapolis, Minnesota

© 2016 by Leighann McCoy

Published by Bethany House Publishers
11400 Hampshire Avenue South
Bloomington, Minnesota 55438
www.bethanyhouse.com

Bethany House Publishers is a division of
Baker Publishing Group, Grand Rapids, Michigan

Printed in the United States of America

Library of Congress Control Number: 2016930577

ISBN 978-0-7642-1755-5

Cover design by Rob Williams, InsideOutCreativeArts

Author is represented by Smith Management Partners, LLC.

16 17 18 19 20 21 22   7 6 5 4 3 2 1

Dedicated to my husband, Tom

You were wise enough to know that having children might be harder than either of us could ever imagine and patient enough to battle with me through infertility to conceive them.

You've been steadfast, passionate, compassionate, and strong as both a godly father and husband.

We cry, we laugh, we bow down, and we rise up . . . together.

Mikel, Kaleigh, and TJ are God's best idea for us! And we're His best idea for them.

God's got some strange ideas.

Here's to His thoughts and not ours, His ways and not ours.

Here's to "three for three" for the glory of God!

"A bruised reed he will not break,
and a smoldering wick he will
not snuff out, till he has brought
justice through to victory."
Matthew 12:20

Home is
Where you can be silent and still be heard
Where you can ask and find out who you are
Where people laugh with you about yourself
Where sorrows are divided and joys are multiplied
Where we share and love and grow

My mother-in-law, Sterline McCoy, gave me a cross-stitched wall hanging with this poem on it. May God grant us homes like this.

Contents

Contents

Introduction

If you are reading this, you either know spiritual warfare is real or you are curious as to whether it might be. But that's not really why you picked up this book. The real reason is that the people you love most are causing you the most grief (or you are afraid they might cause you grief in the future). If you introduced them to me, I'd call them your family. You might call them crazy. We might both be tempted to label our families "dysfunctional." I haven't met a "normal" family yet. But more than anything, you want to know there is hope for your prodigal, for your child or children, grandchildren, and/or for your spouse, and I want to shout to you, "THERE IS!"

This is a book about hope. It's a book about victory and success. It's also a book about spiritual warfare.

Wow! Even the words make my skin crawl. I'm not one of those people who thinks there's a demon behind every smart remark your preteen utters. I never watch movies that exalt spiritual darkness. But I do believe in a fourth or fifth dimension that Scripture calls "the heavenlies," and I know that these places are very real. I have put my faith in God, who gets involved in the details of my life. And as I've grown to experience Him more, I've also come up-close-and-personal with the "roaring lion" (1 Peter 5:8), who is intent on stealing my faith and destroying my witness.

I'm here to tell you that what you are experiencing in your family is not the normal stuff of life. It's a battle—a spiritual battle—and there is a way for you to win this fight. If you are not experiencing the battle yet, you will, and I'm glad you have the foresight to get yourself prepared.

I intend to tell you in this book how to win.

You may want to shout aloud, "How can you be so sure?!"

Here's how. I serve the Commander in Chief of heaven's armies, and He's already won this war. The God whom I serve has no equal in power. His understanding is perfect (meaning that there isn't anything lurking in the shadows that He's not already fully aware of). He's not only strong, He is also crazy in love with you. And because He loves you, He's going to teach you how to fight to win. The almost laughable thing about this is that He's going to use me to guide your training.

I'm not a drill sergeant, nor am I a decorated war hero. I'm just a pastor's wife (of all things) from Middle Tennessee, who's lived through her share of battles and learned how to fight.

When my children heard me say I was about to start writing another book on spiritual warfare, they exclaimed, "Are you kidding me?!" They are bracing themselves for attack. In fact, we are recruiting prayer partners to stand in the gap for us as I take on this project. My husband, Tom, just smiles knowingly, and I often shake my head and mutter under my breath, "What am I thinking?"

Then I remember that we worship what we fear most, and I am determined to allow my esteem of God to override my fear of the Enemy of our souls. I'm also determined to trust Him more and to stand on the tried-and-true fact that every attack from the Enemy brings with it a divine invitation from the heart of God to know by experience what Love does. This was the theme of my first book on spiritual warfare, *Spiritual Warfare for Women*.

When I came to my "laughing place" (an eighty-year-old farmhouse in the North Carolina mountains where I go to write) to begin my work on *Spiritual Warfare for Women*, my daughter (eighteen at the time) interrupted that getaway by moving into an apartment with her boyfriend. Just a few weeks later we discovered she was pregnant. That was only the beginning of what has become our new "normal." But during those enemy attacks, I tested the things I thought I'd learned about spiritual warfare and found them to be true. I put those truths on paper. I could pretend that was easy and bolster your confidence in me, but to be quite honest, I birthed that "baby" amid some serious moans and groans. But in the process, I discovered a whole lot more about God than I would have ever learned any other way. I wrote about most of those things in *A Woman's Guide to Hearing God's Voice*. That manuscript was written while I fought a recurrence of colon cancer that involved having half my liver removed and six months of chemotherapy.

So as I stare at my signed contract with Bethany House and sit in front of the wood stove with my computer before me, once again at my laughing place, I am closing my eyes and whispering a prayer: "Dear Lord, stop me right now if this isn't where you're going and please, please, *pleeease* bring those I love to the other side intact."

With that said, let me tell you what I plan to show you in this book. Spiritual warfare is real. We live on a battlefield; our life on earth is like a deployment. But victory is yours, not just in the end but in the now. I don't care how hopeless your situation seems, don't be snookered into thinking you cannot win these battles! Don't worry if you don't know how; that's why you're reading this book.

There are many battlefronts in this spiritual war, but there is one battlefield that wounds us deeper than any other, and that is the battle the Enemy levels against our homes. In this book, I intend to tell you how to win the battles that rage against your family.

I'm going to start by explaining what spiritual warfare is and why it continues today. I'm going to clarify for you the legal transaction that took place when Jesus died on the cross for your sins. And then I'm going to explain the effect of that legal transaction on your life now. After that I'm going to show you what you're doing wrong. Don't worry, there are only three things, and once you know what these are, I'm going to tell you how to fix them. After that I'll share three truths that will give you a definite advantage on the battlefield. These things are true whether you know them or not, so Satan can't do a thing about their reality. He can, however, keep you confused over these truths so that you don't use them to your advantage. Once you understand these truths, you will also gain tools to implement them in the trenches during the fight. I'm praying already that you don't lose this book just before you read these chapters. The devil doesn't want you to know what I've written there.

Knowledge is power. In the next part of this book, I will share what I've come to know about the Enemy's targeted attack on our thought lives and show you that the battle really is "all in your head." This will lead to a discussion of the "high places" we tend to construct when we put our confidence in something or someone other than God. You will learn to define the arguments, pretensions, and strongholds that must be destroyed in order to take back possession of blessings and guarantees the Enemy may have stolen from you. You will learn about three of the incredible divine powers God has given us to demolish the devil's strongholds. At the end of this section, you will learn how to operate the divine weapons He's provided.

In part 5 of the book, I will identify your children's vulnerable places based on their life stages and then help you create a strategy for making them strong. In part 6, I will discuss several issues that are common to families today. While these issues aren't necessarily spiritual attacks, the devil does use them to get an upper hand in our families. If you are in crisis right now, flip through part 6 and see if you are struggling with one of these issues. You might want to read that chapter first and then read the rest of the book.

I originally had an appendix planned, but decided that these resources would be more accessible to you online. Therefore, you can find some incredible tools for your family's spiritual arsenal on my website at www.LeighannMcCoy.com/SpiritualWarfareTools

and at bakerpublishinggroup.com/books/spiritual-warfare-for
-your-family/378360. These tools include several more issues that
are common to families, a downloadable worksheet for developing your family's core values, and links to some of the best sex
education tools for parents.

If you are still reading this, then I know you are serious about
winning the war in your home. I've got a few warnings and promises: I warn you that you may cry a time or two while you read
this book. I promise you will laugh. I warn you that you might
be stretched and even broken in this journey. I promise you that
when you arrive at the end you will be stronger than ever before.
I warn you that it's going to get messy (most likely it already has).
I promise you your messes are the special ingredient in God's
miracles. It's time to win these battles. Are you ready?

PART 1

The Battle Is Real

We live in a perpetual battlefield. . . . The wars among the nations on earth are mere popgun affairs compared to the fierceness of battle in the spiritual unseen world. This invisible spiritual conflict is waged around us incessantly and unremittingly. Where the Lord works, Satan's forces hinder [God's work]; where angel beings carry out divine directives, the devils rage. All this comes about because the powers of darkness press their counterattack to recapture the ground held for the glory of God.

—Billy Graham, *Angels*

1

You're Not Crazy; There Really Is a Battle Waging

It was 2:32 a.m. I'd just finished swabbing up the blood from my nosebleed. I was so weak from not eating that I could hardly keep my hands from shaking as I tried to sip the lukewarm water I'd put on the nightstand when I went to bed. I hadn't swallowed anything cold for more than two months. The chemo I was receiving created a heightened sensitivity to the cold, stole my appetite, gave me high blood pressure, and left me feeling nauseous and achy. I was sick, I was tired, and I felt half dead.

I prayed to God, "Am I going to die from this cancer?"

His answer was unexpected, as it often is. Instead of saying, *"No, Leighann, you're not dying. You're going to be okay. I'm going to let you live a long and prosperous life,"* He said, *"You can if you'd like. You can leave all this behind and come to where there is no chemo, no suffering, no heartache, and no pain. You can join me where I am and live forever!"*

"Or," He continued, *"you can stay on the battlefield a bit longer. But know that if you do, it's going to be hard, very hard. Your life is going to involve suffering and disappointment."*

His answer sounded much more like an invitation than anything else. It was as if God were inviting me to go ahead and play my get-out-of-jail-free card!

I contemplated my response. I could leave and be done or I could hang around and stop whining.

Seriously, I could stay and choose to be used by God, spent for the well-being of those I loved and those God loved, or I could go on to eternity, where it really doesn't matter so much whether you live ten, fifty, or ninety years on earth in comparison to the ten thousand years that make up the first season in heaven.

I chose to stay. I thanked God for His kindness and submitted to His warning. Now when those no-good, horrible, terrible, very bad things happen, I am reminded that God assured me they would. I am on assignment. I am here to fight.

We are soldiers living in hostile territory. The day will come when we get to go home, but until then we have battles to win.

As you read this book you are going to discover that not only are your battles real, they can be won, and you can experience the victory of God as you're winning them.

Let's start by defining spiritual warfare in general and then in the way it manifests itself in your home.

Spiritual Warfare Defined

Spiritual warfare is the ongoing resistance that Satan launches against God by exerting his arrogant desire to be God.

It is real.

It is vicious, violent, vile, and brutal.

Until you discover what a warrior you are!

The war began in the heavenlies and will end there as well. But it's fought mostly on earth today, and your family is smack-dab in the middle of the battle. Satan has a long history of attacking families. Cain and Abel, Noah and his sons, Sarah and Hagar, Joseph and his brothers—the list goes on and on.

Tony Evans, a respected pastor and frequent teacher on the subject of spiritual warfare, said this:

> We have to help people understand the cause-effect relationship. There frequently is a strong link between the spiritual and physical. That is, what we are dealing with in the physical realm often can be determined by what is taking place in the spiritual realm. Our failure to deal with the spiritual cause of the problems we encounter can really mess us up.[1]

Perhaps you purchased this book because you are dealing with some "messed-up" stuff in your life. I'm here to assure you that you are not alone. There is a distinct connection between the experiences, circumstances, difficulties, and relationships in your life and the spiritual world.

In fact, Jesus warned us that we would be at war with this world if we chose to follow Him.

> If the world hates you, remember that it hated me first. The world would love you as one of its own if you belonged to it, but you are no longer part of the world. I chose you to come out of the world, so it hates you. Do you remember what I told you? "A slave is not greater than the master." Since they persecuted me, naturally they will persecute you. And if they had listened to me, they would listen to you. They will do all this to you because of me, for they have rejected the one who sent me.
>
> John 15:18–21 NLT

The world will hate you. You can expect persecution, and both the people and the situations in your life can be used by the forces of evil to distract, discourage, and defeat you. Because the family was ordained by God as the single most important building block for human society, and the family of God (the church) takes its structure and form from the structure and form of the family unit, the devil targets families for attack.

Because there is God the Father and Jesus the Son of God, when relationships between children and their fathers are not what they are designed to be, the world cannot understand the relationship between God the Father and Jesus the Son. When we are "born again," we are born into the family of God, where once again God is the Father and we are His sons and daughters. We are joint heirs with Christ (Romans 8:15–17). When the relationships between children and parents are destroyed, the world cannot understand the privilege of being children of God.

Not only does Satan seek to confuse biblical truth, but if he can gain a foothold in your home, Satan can distract your attention from the work God has for you to do. He can discourage you and drain your emotional energy so that you lose the strength to persevere. And his main objective is to destroy your testimony. Satan messes with your family because he knows that your home gives him ready access to your heart.

Satan's attack on the family takes three approaches. He targets the marriage for attack, he targets the relationship between parents and children for attack, and he targets the relationship among siblings for attack. On these three fronts, Satan works to tear apart and devour love and trust, devotion to God, and effective witness to the world.

You are not crazy. There is a definite relationship between what you are experiencing in your family and what is going on in the spiritual realm. My goal is to help you recognize those relationships so that you can put them in perspective, understand the bigger picture, and win the battles for your home. In these first few chapters, I'm going to start by explaining how the war began, then we are going to discuss spiritual authority and how that relates to the legal transaction that took place on the cross, and after that I will answer this question: "If the war's been won, why am I fighting today?"

Some Messed-Up Stuff

I mentioned before that you might be dealing with some messed-up stuff in your home. I know it's hard and you're tired and you're starving for answers. It's my prayer that you find them as you read this book. I'm going to be sharing a lot of foundational truths as we start out, for these truths will uproot the lies that create the strongholds that leave you powerless and ineffective on the battlefield. I urge you to take a deep breath and resist the urge to rush through these chapters. I promise that I'll sprinkle in some practical application and laughter along the way. As far as I know, I am the only author of a spiritual warfare book that talks about skinny-dipping (see *Spiritual Warfare for Women*).

But I know there are times when you need something to do right now. If that is where you find yourself today, go to part 6 in this book and find the collection of chapters dealing with fourteen common issues families are facing. While my list is far from exhaustive, I've tried to include the major issues Satan uses to destroy families. If the issue you are facing is not included in this book, go to www. LeighannMcCoy.com/SpiritualWarfareTools to find several more critical issues. In each chapter, I briefly describe the issue, then provide you with four action steps you can take, five Scripture promises to include in your spiritual arsenal as you go to battle for your family, and a prayer to pray daily as you read this book. So if your heart is breaking and you need a strategy to embrace right away, take up the sword and go to battle while learning how to fight more effectively.

QUESTIONS TO CONSIDER

At the end of each chapter, I will include questions to consider. Use these to apply the truths presented in that chapter to your specific battle. If you are reading this book in a small group, use these questions to spur discussion.

1. How are the struggles in your home distracting you from God?
2. What spiritual truths are you having a hard time believing?
3. Do you believe you are fighting spiritual forces? Why, or why not?

4. If you were to tweet a statement from this chapter, which of these would you tweet?

- Not only are your battles real, they can be won and you can experience the victory of God as you're winning them.
- Both the people and the situations in your life can be used by the forces of evil to distract, discourage, and defeat you.
- You are not crazy.

2

Did God Create the Devil?

You may be wondering where Satan and spiritual warfare come from. Here's a question that used to scare me: "Did God create the devil?" I found the answer in Isaiah 54:16: "It is I who have created the destroyer to wreak havoc."

Yes, God created the devil.

But just because God created the devil doesn't mean that God created evil. Satan chose that for himself. The reason some have an issue with God creating the devil is that they can't reconcile the creation of evil with the holiness of God. God did not create evil. He generously gave angels and humans free will. Consider my children. Did I create my daughters and son? My husband and I conceived them. I carried them to full term and gave birth to each one. Without us, Mikel, Kaleigh, and TJ wouldn't be here. We reared them. But are we responsible for the choices they are making now?

The fact that God created the devil doesn't bother me anymore. Instead, it encourages me. While spiritual warfare is the struggle between God and Satan, it isn't a desperate struggle between two equal but opposing forces. There's never a moment in time when

God is concerned that Satan might defeat Him, that he might get the upper hand, or that Satan might topple God from His throne.

God is the Creator of the universe.

Satan is a created being.

God is head over all authority, power, dominion, and title that can be given (Ephesians 1:20–23). God rules over all of creation from the tiniest microbe to the most powerful spiritual forces. He is the microscopic God and the macrocosmic God.

Satan is the most powerful ruler of evil spiritual forces. He has limited jurisdiction as he roams the earth. He is not equal to God in power, rule, or authority. Satan is subject to God, and his destiny has already been determined. (Read Revelation 19 and 20 to learn more about what happens to the devil in the end.)

God created Lucifer (a heavenly name for Satan) as an archangel in heaven. He was equal in power and either equal to or perhaps one step above the position of the other archangels who still lead the heavenly hosts. Lucifer exercised his own free will and chose to rebel against heaven's glory.

When he rebelled, a third of heaven's angels rebelled with him. Most likely these were the angels who served under Lucifer's God-given authority. Their loyalty to Lucifer was apparently greater than their loyalty to God. Today these former angels are demons. Like Satan, demons are spiritual beings with supernatural power equal to that of the angels.

Lucifer allowed pride to compel him to rise up against God (see Isaiah 14:12–15). He was soundly defeated in that revolt. Revelation 12 speaks of the heavenly defeat of the "dragon" and the demons.

This uprising and subsequent defeat of Lucifer and a third of heaven's armies happened somewhere either before Genesis 1:1 or between 1:1 and 3:1, when Satan, in the form of the serpent, appeared on the earth to Eve and Adam.

Spiritual warfare became personal to us when Eve chose to listen to the serpent and she and Adam traded their lives of perfect communion with God for lives of self-rule and slavery to sin. When Adam and Eve made this transaction from God-rule to self-rule, the spiritual order that God had ordained "in the beginning" was destroyed. In fact, Satan's first attack was on the family. Eve offered Adam the fruit, and Adam blamed Eve when God asked him to give an account of his sin. Trust and innocence were lost. They were replaced by fear, self-consciousness, blame, and shame.

An Understanding of Spiritual Authority, Rule, and Dominion

Let's talk for a minute about authority. Authority can be defined as the power to give orders, make decisions, and command obedience. Authority can only be given to someone if the person giving it truly has that authority to give. For instance, I can tell my son that he has my permission to take his finance test with an open book and turn it in three days later than the rest of the students in the class. I can tell him to do this because I love him and want him to do well on his test. But if he does it, he will still pay the consequences to his professor for not taking his test on time. I don't have any authority over what goes on in my son TJ's finance class. Only his professor has that power.

This is an important truth to remember as you are laying the foundation for winning spiritual battles in your home. God has supreme authority over all His creation. He made it. He had authority to give dominion (or the power of control) to whomever He wanted to give it. And God chose to give the power to rule over all of creation to mankind.

> So God created mankind in his own image, in the image of God he created them; male and female he created them. God blessed them and said to them, "Be fruitful and increase in number; fill the earth *and subdue it. Rule over* the fish of the sea and the birds in the sky and over every living creature that moves on the ground."
>
> Genesis 1:27–28, emphasis added

29

God saw fit to give mankind the power to rule over all He had made. God, who had all authority, gave us complete authority to rule over all the rest of creation. Even knowing what would happen, along with authority, God also gave mankind free will—the opportunity to choose obedience or not. He didn't make puppets; God made companions when He created us. Because God gave us free will, He chose to set boundaries on himself. Have you ever considered this incredible truth?

Your free will sets boundaries (self-imposed boundaries) on God. He is perfect, and therefore God always does the right thing. Out of His perfection, He will never superimpose His will or His ways on those who resist Him. This is an important truth to ponder, and it will impact your effectiveness in fighting battles in your home. We will discuss free will throughout this book and in detail later. For now, let the seed of this truth germinate in your mind.

With free will comes personal responsibility. Adam and Eve both tried to shirk this personal responsibility when Adam blamed Eve and Eve blamed the serpent for the predicament they found themselves in when God confronted them with their sin. The moment Adam and Eve ate from the fruit of the Tree of Knowledge of Good and Evil, a legal transaction took place in the spiritual realm. Satan, the defeated leader of the heavenly rebellion, gained control of God's glorious creation; he gained access to the souls of people. Satan knew that if Adam and Eve disobeyed God, they would no longer live in oneness with God. Their sin separated them from God, and once they were separated from God, they lost His divine power and wisdom to keep the world in order. Mankind also lost position in heavenly rank. Rather than be with God in the position that is above all other powers, mankind fell. We landed in the place where we were created, earth. Because we lost our position with God, we lost power over the other spiritual powers.

Mankind still functions as the crown of creation with superior intellect and therefore rules over the natural world, but spiritually speaking, our minds are clouded and our power is limited. Jesus stated this truth plainly when He said, "Apart from me you can do nothing" (John 15:5). Adam and Eve exchanged their intimate personal relationship with God for a bite of fruit. They chose to be separated from Him, and therefore they separated themselves from His wisdom to rule the earth and from His spiritual authority and power to carry out His plans.

Not only did Adam and Eve fall from grace, but all of creation fell with them. Control over all of God's creation went from God to Satan through the channel of their sin. And with that transaction, Satan brought the war against God to earth. Ever since that fateful day in the Garden of Eden, all of God's creation fell into disarray and earth became a global battlefield. People still have dominance, but if we are separated from God, our rule of the earth is contaminated and usurped by sin and Satan. If any man (or woman) is reunited with God through salvation, he is restored to his original position in the heavenlies, has access to God's power, and is able to rule the earth again empowered by righteousness and God. But even then, he cannot escape his adversary, whose intent is to hinder his effectiveness.

While mankind, beasts, trees, birds, mountains, and all that was created continued to exist in the form that God created them to be—human nature became sin. With the infection of sin, death, deterioration, and destruction became a part of life. All that goes with all of that—heartache, hatred, prejudice, despair, and so much more—wreaked havoc on earth and transformed what God called "very good" into chaos.

Now, thousands of years later, we've come into a world that faintly resembles the glory of God but has been sorely distorted for millennia. Where once mankind and all of creation shouted to the glory of God, it merely whispers now. The hope for our world today rests in us, Christ's followers, who are seeking to live in a fallen world with resurrection power.

Spiritual warfare began in heaven. The rebellion was brought to earth's battlefield when Adam and Eve exercised their freedom to choose and chose poorly. The battle continues today because God loves people. As long as God cares, people matter. And as long as people matter to God, Satan's opposition must be addressed.

That is how the war got started.

Why Your Home Is a Battlefield

Today, that battle rages in your home because you and your family members are impacted by sin's power. When rebellion, selfishness, addictions, lies, and immorality rule, your "home sweet home" suffers the effects of war. At the heart of every conflict there is brokenness between a person and his/her Creator.

At the very heart of every conflict is this: Rather than looking to God for all that we need, we choose to look to ourselves. Sin's nature is characterized by an insatiable desire to be independent of God. Just like Satan, we want to be gods of our own lives, our own relationships, our own destinies. We want to be "like God." When we rebel against God, we are embracing Satan's agenda. It's the same rebellion that Lucifer led in the heavenlies.

But there is hope! The war's been won! And in this book I'm going to tell you how to release the victory that is yours in your home.

A Powerful Prayer to Pray

I have much more to say about this prayer I'm about to share with you, but for now I want to give it to you so that you can take the first steps necessary to experience victory in your home. Richard Foster wrote this prayer and called it the prayer of relinquishment. The first and often most resistant obstacle you face when gearing up for spiritual war is self: self-will, self-rule, self-reliance, self-sufficiency, selfishness, self, self, self. This prayer will help you break through the barrier of your most familiar foe.

> *Today, O Lord, I yield myself to you.*
> *May your will be my delight today.*

May you have perfect sway in me.
May your love be the pattern of my living.
I surrender to you my hopes, my dreams, my ambitions.
Do with them what you will, when you will, as you
will.
I place into your loving care my family, my friends, my
future.
Care for them with a care that I can never give.
I release into your hands my need to control, my craving
for status, my fear of obscurity.
Eradicate the evil, purify the good, and establish your
kingdom on earth.
For Jesus' sake, amen.[1]

Make this prayer your own and discover the power of it.

QUESTIONS TO CONSIDER

1. Why did you pick up this book?
2. Which sin is fueling your war? Rebellion? Selfishness? Pride? Deception? (There might be more than one.)
3. Whose heart is most affected by the battle you are fighting in your home?
4. What questions do you want answered as you fight your battles?

3

When and How Was the War Won, and Why Do We Fight Today?

This is the part of spiritual warfare that always confused me. What exactly did it mean for Jesus to win the war? And if Jesus won the war on the cross, why do we fight today?

Wars are fought over issues of authority. Who has the right to do what . . . when . . . and where? That's what we establish by fighting and conquering our enemies. Peace treaties answer these questions: Who's in charge? What are they in charge of? When do they take charge? What is the extent of their power and authority?

Spiritual warfare is no different. In spiritual warfare God is in charge. He rules the heavens and the earth; He's always been in charge and He always will be. His power and authority are supreme. But with that said, the supreme authority of God is still challenged by the wicked schemes of Satan. Satan's pride blinds him to the facts.

Don't ever forget: God is Creator and Supreme Ruler of the universe. Satan was created by God. Because he is a former angel, his power is greater than that of people and lesser than that of God. When Satan enticed Adam and Eve to eat the forbidden fruit, he gained power over them, and the sin nature they chose is the one we get too. We were born into the world with the nature of sinners, living under the influence of our flesh. Scripture says that we lived gratifying the cravings of our sinful nature, following its desires and thoughts (see Ephesians 2:1–3). Apart from Christ, our lives are vulnerable to the "ruler of the kingdom of the air" (Satan).

As a result of Adam and Eve's disobedience, they were separated from God and at the same time joined more tightly to the earth. With this heaven-release and earth-tie, Satan gained powerful access over them. The earth-tie that we have causes us to be enticed by our own flesh and by the deception of the devil. This separation from God is a powerful thing, and for centuries mankind was enslaved by the power of sin. Sin delivered death. God warned Adam and Eve this would happen (Genesis 2:17).

But none of this caught God off guard; He had a plan for that. Let's look at John 1, especially verse 14.

"The *Word* became flesh, and dwelt among us" (NASB, emphasis mine).

The Word that was "in the beginning" was the same Word that became flesh and dwelt among us. No wonder the angels sang! God sent Jesus from heaven to earth. The Son of God entered earth to reclaim what had been taken away. Jesus came to restore relationship between us and God. He came down to lift us up. Jesus is the manifest presence of God. He is the complete revelation of God's holiness and therefore His glory. When Jesus was here, He was God walking, talking, interacting, and living among us.

Emmanuel literally means "God with us."

Jesus became one of us but without the death sentence. Since Jesus was without sin, He didn't have to experience death at all. He certainly didn't deserve to die. He could have stayed in heaven with God and ignored the tragic condition of the human soul. But instead, "he gave up his divine privileges [and his exalted position in heaven] . . . and was born as a human being [with all the limitations of an earth suit] . . . and died a criminal's death on a cross" (Philippians 2:7–8 NLT).

We deserve to die, for we all sin, and our mortal, earthly bodies must die. Jesus' earthly body didn't have to die. But rather than avoid death, Jesus willingly yielded himself to it. In life and in death Jesus set His mind and His heart on the will of God. The heart and will of God sent Him to the cross. Jesus chose to offer himself up as the perfect sacrifice for us. No one could do for us what Jesus did, for all others are stained by sin and therefore not worthy to pay sin's price. For the sacrifice to have the power to save and to be accepted by the holiness of God, it had to be perfect and without blemish. The sin He bore on the cross was our sin, not His.

An Understanding of the Glory of God

Let's take a minute to define the *glory of God*. For spiritual warfare has at its core an arrogant denial of and rebellion against the *glory of God*.

What is the glory of God? My definition is this: The glory of God is anything God does that demonstrates/expresses/reveals/shines the light on *who* He is! The glory of God is the undeniable expression of God. Pastor and author John Piper says it much better than I do. He defines the glory of God by comparing the holiness of God with His glory.

> The holiness of God is, I think, his being in a class by himself in his perfection and greatness and worth. . . . His holiness is what he is as God that nobody else is. It is his quality of perfection that can't be improved upon, that can't be imitated, that is incomparable, that determines all that he is and is determined by nothing from outside him. It signifies his infinite worth, his intrinsic, infinite worth, his intrinsic, infinite value.
>
> Now, when Isaiah 6:3 says that angels are crying: "Holy, holy, holy is the Lord God almighty," the next thing they say is this:

"The whole earth is full of his . . ." and you might have expected him to say holiness. And he doesn't say holiness. He says "glory."

Intrinsically holy, intrinsically holy, intrinsically holy and the whole earth is full of his glory from which I stab at a definition by saying the glory of God is the manifest beauty of his holiness. It is the going public of his holiness. It is the way he puts his holiness on display for people to apprehend. So the glory of God is the holiness of God made manifest [visible, apparent].[1]

When John (the apostle, not Piper) said, "We have seen his glory, the glory of the one and only Son, who came from the Father" (John 1:14), he was saying that Jesus was the visible, apparent, manifest expression of God.

So Jesus came to earth with a mission. His mission was to reveal God's glory to God's people and *also* to reclaim mankind for himself. (See John 17, the prayer Jesus prayed at the end of His earthly ministry.)

This is what Jesus did when He, the perfect, sinless, holy manifestation of the glory of God, chose to obey God and become the perfect, sinless, holy sacrifice so that He could pay the ransom—the wages, the price tag—for our sin. Jesus died to make a legal transaction in the heavenlies that restored mankind to God's original intent. God's original intent for mankind was that we would be His intimate companions *and* executors of His will on earth.

Jesus' death on the cross, an act of obedience by the perfect, sinless representation of God on earth, allowed the grace of God to satisfy His holiness and reestablished God's ability to be intimately connected to mankind. Basically, God "bought us back" from Satan's power over us. God did this because He loves us. It's as simple as that.

When Jesus was crucified, He satisfied the wrath of God. Jesus became sin so that the holiness and glory of God could express its judgment on sin while exercising His merciful love for mankind. God's love for you compelled Him to send His own Son to take your place in death so that you could be restored to God's original intent for your life: "For God so loved the world that he gave his one and only Son, that whoever believes in him shall not perish but have eternal life" (John 3:16).

When Jesus was resurrected from the dead, He established victory over death. With His resurrection, Jesus proved that since sin's price was paid, sin no longer held the power of death. The chains of death were broken because the wrath of God was satisfied. The resurrection of Christ is the victory in the war! With Jesus' resurrection from the dead, the way was opened for all to be reunited with God in the heavenlies with Christ.

"Where, O death, is your sting?" (1 Corinthians 15:55).

Listen to how Paul put this truth to the followers of Christ in Rome:

> If death got the upper hand through one man's wrongdoing, can you imagine the breathtaking recovery life makes, sovereign life, in those who grasp with both hands this wildly extravagant life-gift, this grand setting-everything-right, that the one man Jesus Christ provides?
>
> Here it is in a nutshell: Just as one person did it wrong and got us in all this trouble with sin and death, another person did it right and got us out of it. But more than just getting us out of trouble, he got us into life! One man said no to God and put many people in the wrong; one man said yes to God and put many in the right.
>
> All that passing laws against sin did was produce more lawbreakers. But sin didn't, and doesn't, have a chance in competition with the aggressive forgiveness we call *grace*. When it's sin versus grace, grace wins hands down. All sin can do is threaten us with death, and that's the end of it. Grace, because God is putting everything together again through the Messiah, invites us into life—a life that goes on and on and on, world without end.
>
> Romans 5:17–21 THE MESSAGE

Because Jesus paid sin's penalty by suffering death on the cross, we get to enter into a personal relationship with God. Then, because Jesus resurrected from the dead, we know that all the Bible's promises of eternal life are YES!! And death will be swallowed up in LIFE . . . real life, life like we've never known before.

On the cross, the war was won.

Authority over sin was established, victory over death was declared, and just when Satan might have thought he'd gotten the best of God, he suffered complete and utter defeat. Satan lost the war then and there.

So Why Do We Fight Today?

The minute you accepted God's gift of salvation, you transferred from team Satan to team Jesus in the spiritual order of things. You went from being under the rule of the Prince of Darkness to becoming a citizen in the kingdom of God. Your new citizenship lifted you out of the kingdom of darkness and into the kingdom of light. You are now under the rule, authority, protection, and power of the victorious King of Glory (see Ephesians 2:1–10).

You cannot have dual citizenship; with your new "nationality" you rejected the old. The world and God's kingdom are at war with each other. You cannot love them both. When you entered the kingdom, you became an enemy of this world.

But you still live in the world. When God's Spirit entered into your life, you became a sojourner, a pilgrim, a citizen of a different kingdom. Indicators that you are making the transition from your old way of life to the new might include twinges of homesickness (just knowing that where you are is not "home"), a sense of unsettledness, maintaining low-grade dissatisfaction with the way things are, and feeling lonely at times. You are no longer of this world, so you are going to feel a bit like a traveler. In fact, the writer of Hebrews explained in chapter 11 that this is the way all the faithful men and women felt while they lived their lives on earth.

God rules your new kingdom, and He knows the plans He has for your life. They are good plans, plans to prosper and not to harm you, to give you hope and a future (Jeremiah 29:11). God's plans are like His kingdom, they have no end.

This new life in Christ takes some getting used to. Your entire perspective changes, your focal point is different. Don't be alarmed if it takes you a bit of time to get your bearings just right. God's kingdom order and the world's order are two very different things. Jesus spent much of His earthly ministry explaining these differences.

Satan has plans for your life too. They are bad plans. He plans to harm you, to destroy you, and to steal your hope and your future. Be sure that you understand that there are two spiritual forces, opposed to each other, engaging you in a war. Satan is arrogant and he doesn't want to admit defeat. So even though you belong to God, Satan will come after you. When he does, you will either proclaim the name of the Lord by trusting Him or you will profane the name of the Lord by doubting Him, maintaining your affection for the things of this world, even though you profess to know Him. When you do this, you misrepresent God and misconstrue the expression of His glory.

If you have claimed Jesus as your Savior, you are in the fight. There is no middle ground. When the circumstances of life threaten your faith, you either trust God and take Him at His Word, allowing life's trials to press you into Him, or you don't trust God. Without really meaning to do so, you disregard His Word and dismiss yourself from any expectation of seeing Him actively engaged in the details of your life. When you claim to know God personally but choose not to trust Him you profane His name.

Recently I noticed this verse in Psalm 37:23 (NLT): "The Lord directs the steps of the godly. He delights in every detail of their lives."

This truth that God directs my steps and *delights in every detail* of my life is KEY to me! If I didn't embrace this truth, I would not be teaching you how to win the battles for your home.

The Lord directs your steps.

He delights in the details of your life.

On the battlefield today, Satan does everything he can to destroy you. His specific aim is centered on your faith in God. Robert Jeffress said, "Satan hates you and has a terrible plan for your life. If he cannot succeed in robbing you of eternal life, he will do everything in his power to deprive you of the joy, influence, and rewards that come from serving God in this life."[2]

Satan's demons are active in your world today. But in each battle you have a choice. You can get discouraged, become overwhelmed, subject yourself to defeat, and make it look like Satan has the upper hand in your life, *or* you can stand firm, know that you have already won every battle that comes your way, and *trust God* to come through for you.

There Are Limits to What You Can and Cannot Do

As you wrap your head around the reality of the war and the inevitable suffering of this life, understand that there are limits to what you can and cannot do. One of Satan's greatest deceptions lies in our expecting more from ourselves than God expects. Satan uses the seed of eternity God planted in our hearts to woo us into expecting heaven on earth. We will never experience the absolute joy and peace of heaven while on earth. We will, however, experience glimpses of God's glory, and we will enjoy seasons of pure delight. But the absence of sin and suffering will only come when we are released from our earthly lives. It's important to clarify expectations, limitations, and boundaries that exist in our lives.

I've fought cancer, twice. Prior to my initial diagnosis, I never took the time to examine my physical boundaries. It wasn't that I lived without them, it was just that I lived without paying much attention to them.

But ever since the day I heard "You've got cancer," I wake up each morning grateful for life and mindful that it will one day come to an end. That is a gift that cancer gave me.

My life has boundaries. A few weeks ago, my sister died of cancer. I couldn't stop her from dying. Her death brought much grief to my parents and two other sisters. I couldn't do anything about that. I could only grieve with them. My daughter just reminded me that she's an adult now and I can't parent her like I did when she was twelve. She's right, I can't. There are limits to what I can and can't do for her.

After many years of living my adult life, I've also come to recognize my limitations in work and ministry. I know that if I want to write, I'm going to have to monitor my traveling schedule. I am training for a ten-mile run, and my body reminds me that it's not going to respond to exercise today the way it responded twenty-five years ago.

There are limits to what you can and cannot do.

You might not like those limits; you might fight like crazy against them. But nothing is going to change them. You might as well accept your limitations, and accepting them doesn't reflect a lack of faith.

There Is No Limit to God

But there is no limit to God. He is able to do far more than we experience because we don't even begin to comprehend His power, nor do we understand fully His passionate desire to exercise that power in and through our lives.

Psalm 62:11–12 says this: "One thing God has spoken, two things I have heard: 'Power belongs to you, God, and with you, Lord, is unfailing love'; and, 'You reward everyone according to what they have done.'"

God's desire is to demonstrate His love and His power on the platform of your life. Spiritual freedom depends as much on accepting your limits as it does on putting your trust in your limitless God.

The Heart of the Issue in Your Home

At the heart of spiritual warfare is the battle over souls. The souls of your family members are at the heart of the battle in your home. Their victory, and yours, is found in the cross of Christ. We will discuss this more, but for now, I want to share something personal with you.

For several years I've been fighting a battle in my home. I've discussed this battle with great transparency in my books *Spiritual Warfare for Women* and *A Woman's Guide to Hearing God's Voice*, but I've made a commitment not to discuss it here, at least not in detail. However, I do want to share what happened a few weeks ago.

I received a phone call from a distressed mother. She was understandably concerned for her daughter. I told her my father had recently urged me to focus more on the "why" than the "what." She and I both agreed that was great advice, but we wondered exactly what the "why" was.

A few minutes after I hung up the phone, I found a blog post online written by a young woman who'd spent several years of her life breaking her mother's heart. She titled her post "To the Parents of Prodigal Children," and this is what she wrote:

> Love them by helping, as you have opportunity, to expose the lies they are *believing, acting on, feeling* as truth. You can do this by *focusing on the root cause of the sin—their departure from their relationship with God—rather than on the symptoms* of the sin you are seeing in their actions.[3]

At the root of every issue is a disconnect between our loved one and God. Love them, lovingly expose the lies they have chosen to believe, and speak truth into their lives. The irony is you must do the same. If you want to win these battles:

1. Examine your relationship with God.

2. Invite the Holy Spirit to expose the lies you've chosen to believe.

3. Speak truth.

If you will do these three things daily and keep praying the prayer of relinquishment, you will begin to see a difference in your battles.

QUESTIONS TO CONSIDER

1. How does Satan's defeat impact the way you view your struggle?

2. What does your salvation mean to you today?

3. Is there anyone in your home who needs salvation? Pray for him/her now.

PART 2

Never Lose a Battle Again

Christ has left the devil only whatever power our unbelief allows him.

—Heinrich Schlier

4

Three Reasons You're Losing Your Battles

Satan hates you. He hates your worship, he hates your devotion, he hates your prayers, and he hates when you get together with your friends and study the Bible. Because Satan hates you, he orchestrates attacks against you. He finds your vulnerabilities and exploits them. His attacks come in thousands of different ways, but at the core of each one is the intent to convince you to compromise your faith and doubt God. Satan wants you to do the exact opposite of Proverbs 3:5–6: "Trust in the Lord with all your heart and lean not on your own understanding; in all your ways submit to him, and he will make your paths straight."

Satan wants to rewrite the words like this: "Question the Lord and His motives at every turn. Figure it all out yourself. In all your ways ignore God and blaze your own trail."

For an enemy who's been defeated and disarmed, he's a formidable foe because he is a master spinner. He knows how to spin things so that you get all confused, forget God's promises, and live like a pauper when you're the child of the King of Kings. Before

I knew I was in a war, he beat me because I was ignorant. Once I realized that life was a battlefield, I did a bit better. But all too often, this crafty serpent of the ages scored against me and left me limping in retreat to nurse my wounds. I've described my daily combat like this: I used to know just enough to line up on the field and shout the battle cry, even go toe-to-toe with evil . . . and get beaten to a pulp.

Many times I felt like a prisoner of war. I lost plenty of battles. And those losses delivered the rewards of discouragement, disillusionment, and shame.

Why does this happen?

The war's been won!

I serve on the winning team!

I might have learned to live with considerable losses had Satan left my family alone. But when he brought the battle home, the stakes were too high. You can mess with my health, my work, and my friendships, but don't mess with my husband and kids.

I'm going to assume that you feel that way too; that's why you're reading this book. Well come on, my frustrated warrior, I've got a good word (or more) for you today. I'm here to tell you, in these next few chapters, that you can win this battle! Satan doesn't have to have your loved one(s), and you don't have to lose.

Jesus saved you to win.

Jesus has given you everything you need to win every single battle.

You can become a force to be reckoned with on the battlefield. You can fight to win, but first you need to understand the reasons you lose.

Three Reasons We Lose Battles

1. We are confused over who we are in Christ.
2. We are ignorant of how to exercise spiritual authority in our lives.
3. We don't tap into the glorious riches of our spiritual inheritance while we're going to war in the trenches.

Ephesians 1:3–14 addresses these three essential truths. By examining these verses closely and accepting the truth they declare, you will be well on your way to training your mind to win your battles.

> Blessed be the God and Father of our Lord Jesus Christ, who has blessed us in Christ with every spiritual blessing in the heavenly places, even as he chose us in him before the foundation of the world, that we should be holy and blameless before him. In love he predestined us for adoption as sons through Jesus Christ, according to the purpose of his will, to the praise of his glorious grace, with which he has blessed us in the Beloved. In him we have redemption through his blood, the forgiveness of our trespasses, according to the riches of his grace, which he lavished upon us, in all wisdom and insight making known to us the mystery of his will, according to his purpose, which he set forth in Christ as a plan for the fullness of time, to unite all things in him, things in heaven and things on earth.
>
> In him we have obtained an inheritance, having been predestined according to the purpose of him who works all things according to the counsel of his will, so that we who were the first to hope in Christ might be to the praise to his glory. In him you also, when you heard the word of truth, the gospel of your salvation, and believed in him, were sealed with the promised Holy Spirit, who is the guarantee of our inheritance until we acquire possession of it, to the praise of his glory.
>
> ESV

You Have Positional Victory Over Satan

Get your pen out and underline (or highlight on your electronic device) every reference in Ephesians 1:3–14 to your living "in Christ" or "in him." Don't skip over this exercise. This is important.

Most likely you are grieved and concerned over what your son, daughter, or spouse is lacking in their relationship with God. I promise we will get to them in a bit, but for now, recognize that the battle you are fighting has been allowed by the sovereign hand of God to teach you more about who you are *in Christ* and who Christ is *in you*. And the more you understand your position in Christ, the more you will learn to apply the positional victory you have over Satan's attack on you and your family.

You might have found ten or more references to our lives "in Christ." Robertson McQuilkin tells a great story to illustrate the positional victory we have in Christ:

> My sixth-grade buddy and I were having a water-gun fight during school recess. Just as I shot at him, the school bully happened to run between us and caught the stream of water on the side of his head. Twice my size, he could have twisted me into a pretzel with his bare hands, but instead he reached into his pocket and drew out a switchblade knife. Then began the Big Chase. It was chicken to go in the schoolhouse before the bell rang, so I started around the school yard with Big Jim in hot pursuit. Round and round, with all the kids, like some giant swarm of bees, following to see the slaughter. Finally, the saving bell! Into the safety of the classroom, but only for a time. Just as I suspected, when school was out, there he stood guard at the gate. I sneaked out another exit and over backyard fences the four blocks to the safety of home. Every day a different route, till finally I ran out of stratagems. A very lonely Friday afternoon found me disconsolate in a darkened hallway, contemplating my nemesis waiting patiently by the gate. I glanced out the side window, and, to my astonishment, there was a sight I'd never seen before and never since. My father was walking down the sidewalk! Down the side stairs and out to greet him with unaccustomed warmth, I put my hand in his as we marched together past the front gate. "Hi, Jim!" I said with studied nonchalance.[1]

When you put your hand in the hand of Christ, when you walk with Him, you can face your fear and take down your bully. The first sermon I ever heard my husband preach was at his father's church. Tom grew up at First Baptist Church in Dickson, Tennessee, and if he'd stood in the pulpit and sang "The Star-Spangled Banner," I think people would have been saved because of the life transformation the people in the congregation had witnessed in their little PK. But he was preaching a spring revival message, and he got all excited and shouted, "I'm so saved, I could swing three feet over hell on a rotten corn stalk, spit in the devil's eye, and sing 'Victory in Jesus'!" I don't know if that declaration was original with him, but it still makes me smile to remember him saying it.

Tom was expressing his positional victory in Christ. When you were saved, you were united with Christ in the heavenlies with God. God is the Lord of heaven's armies! He is the Lord God Almighty. When Jesus holds you in His hand, His hand is attached to His arm, His arm is attached to His body, and His body sits on a throne right beside His Father God. So *you are there!* Consider this truth:

> Since you have been raised to new life with Christ, set your sights on the realities of heaven, where Christ sits in the place of honor at God's right hand. Think about the things of heaven, not the things of earth. For you died to this life, and your real life is hidden with Christ in God.
>
> Colossians 3:1–3 NLT

You are seated in the heavenlies with Christ! God raised you up to sit there, and He's not going to let you go. From this place, you have supremacy over evil rulers and authorities of the unseen world, mighty powers of this dark world, and evil spirits in the heavenly places (Ephesians 6:12). You are saved! You have power and authority! You rule!

You can have the kind of victory Tom described in his sermon when I was starry-eyed over him way back in the spring of 1986. Go ahead, shout it out: "I'm so saved, I could swing three feet over hell on a rotten corn stalk, spit in the devil's eye, and sing 'Victory in Jesus'!"

You Have Provisional Victory Over Satan

In Ephesians 1:3–14, you also discover the provision God has for you as you go to battle against the Enemy. While this is not an exhaustive list of the spiritual blessings God's given us, it is a great start to a list. Consider keeping an ongoing list of every spiritual blessing that is yours as you read God's Word.

Now make a list of the spiritual blessings Paul lists in these verses. I counted eight.

1.

2.

3.

4.

5.

6.

7.

8.

Receive these blessings by declaring their reality in your life. These blessings give you twelve truths that will sustain you on the battlefield. Read these truth statements aloud.

Truth Statements

1. I am the beneficiary of every spiritual blessing in the heavens.
2. God chose me.
3. I am holy and blameless in His sight.
4. I was predestined for adoption in His family. I am a son/daughter of the King.
5. I am favored by God. He considers me His favorite!
6. I am redeemed.
7. My sins are forgiven.
8. His grace has been lavished on me.
9. God let me in on the mystery of His perfect plan and that is to bring all things together in Christ, my Savior and Lord.

10. God reveals His secrets to me.
11. God chose me to show the world He is the same today as He was in the days Scripture was written.
12. I am His inheritance, and I have the person of the Holy Spirit living in me as a guarantee that I am His and He is mine for now and for all eternity.

This is who you are in Christ, and some of the glorious riches of your inheritance. The Bible is filled with lists of God's glorious riches. His provisions include the most advanced battle gear ever. When you put on the full armor of God, you will be able to stand your ground. And after the dust from the battle settles, you will discover that you have won.

Spiritual Battle Gear

As a spiritual soldier, you are equipped with spiritual armor. Be familiar with this gear, and be sure to wear it daily. As long as you are breathing, you are deployed. When you stop breathing, God has called you home. Since you are deployed, the enemy could be anywhere at anytime. Just as our deployed soldiers wear their combat gear when they leave the FOB (Forward Operating Base), so should you. Here are the pieces of your spiritual armor according to Ephesians 6:14–17:

1. Belt of truth
2. Breastplate of righteousness
3. Shoes of the gospel of peace
4. Shield of faith
5. Helmet of salvation
6. Sword of the Spirit

God has given you all you need to win. Learn to lay hold of His provisions. We will talk more about your provisions in this book.

If Satan's Been Defeated, Why Am I Losing These Battles?

You lose your battles when you forget to exercise your positional victory. You also lose your battles when you fail to apply your provisional victory by using the glorious riches of your inheritance. If you're living defeated, it's because you've forgotten the privilege of your position and the power of your provision.

Memorize Colossians 3:1–3, and print the twelve truth statements on an index card. Declare these truths daily until their reality rules over all other thoughts that invade your mind. In this way you will increase your battle skills because, as I reveal in the next chapter, the battle really is all in your head.

QUESTIONS TO CONSIDER

1. Have you made your handwritten list? If not, make it now.
2. What is so powerful about your position in Christ?
3. Do you believe you can win your battles?

5

The Battle Really Is All in Your Head

Is the battle really all in your head?

Yes, it is.

That's the only place it can be! Don't ever forget this fact.

You don't war against people, but against principalities (Ephesians 6:12); and you don't fight circumstances but your interpretation of those circumstances. The devil's got nothing to throw at you that can touch Christ who is in you, so he resorts to trickery and deception, and the only place those tactics work is in your head.

Neil Anderson said this:

> You are free in Christ, but you will be defeated if the devil can deceive you into believing you are nothing more than a sin-sick product of your past. Nor can Satan do anything about your position in Christ, but if he can deceive you into believing what the Scripture says isn't true, you will live as though it isn't. *People are in bondage to the lies they believe.*[1]

The devil defeats you on the battlefield of your mind by distorting truth and convincing you of lies. The only power these lies have is the power you give them when you respond to them as if they were truth. This strategy of deception works. History has been altered by men and armies who believed lies.

In Sun Tzu's famous book *The Art of War* he states, "All warfare is based on deception."

The Power of Deception

Just north of my home, in Brentwood, Tennessee, there is a statue that really should be removed. It is of Nathan Bedford Forrest, the famed Confederate general who was also a leader in the Ku Klux Klan. It was erected (interestingly enough) by one of the attorneys who defended the assassin of Martin Luther King Jr., another good reason it should be removed. You can see this eyesore when you travel north on Interstate 65, just off the right side of the road midway between exits 74 and 78. Even though I would be in favor of removing this ugly statue, Nathan Bedford Forrest does give me a great illustration of the deceptive power of the enemy in war.

According to Maurice D'Aoustand's article "Hoodwinked During America's Civil War: Confederate Military Deception," on July 13, 1862, Nathan Bedford Forrest led his 1,400 horsemen to the tiny town of Murfreesboro, Tennessee, and captured Brigadier Gen. Thomas T. Crittenden and his guard. After many of their regiment were captured, the 9th Michigan assembled and could have possibly fought a fierce battle, but under the truce flag, Forrest duped Lieutenant Colonel Parkhurst into believing that the rest of Crittenden's forces had been captured and that no quarter would be given to the 9th if they continued to resist. Parkhurst put the decision to fight to a vote and his troops chose to surrender to Forrest.

Forrest then went north, where he faced the 3rd Minnesota and their four-gun battery. Since Forrest had no artillery of his own, all he had was his deception. So he issued his "no quarter" terms to Colonel Henry Lester, the commander of the 3rd Minnesota. Lester demanded proof that the 9th Michigan had surrendered. Forrest gave Lester an escorted tour of now rebel-controlled Murfreesboro, and Lester surrendered.

One of Forrest's favorite sayings was "Keep up the scare."

Forrest was outnumbered and out-armed, but he defeated his enemy with the power of deception. In researching this, I discovered that the Confederates were adept at duping the enemy. They built campfires and left drummers to play across empty fields to give the impression that troops were camped and ready to face battle in the morning. P. G. T. Beauregard had an empty train drive back and forth all night long with each stop theatrically welcomed with whooping and hollering so that the federal forces would imagine that reinforcements were arriving throughout the night when in reality he was escorting his troops out of a dire situation.[2]

When an enemy is both outnumbered and out-armed, his best weapon is deception! The devil is both defeated and disarmed, but he still wins victories in our lives through his cunning use of deception. I can almost hear him rally his demons right now with "Keep up the scare."

Let me see if I can explain how this works by sharing a personal illustration.

When I was in college, a group of my friends and I went on a weekend retreat. I was canoeing with a friend who was deathly afraid of water because he didn't know how to swim. His canoe tipped and even though he was wearing a life jacket, he panicked. As I tried to give him reassurance that he would not drown on my watch, I stuck my paddle in the water and discovered that although it was murky, it was only waist deep. Stifling my laughter, I shouted out, "Darryl, stand up!"

Darryl was battling a lie, but as long as he thought it was the truth he struggled. Once he realized the truth, Darryl overcame his fear and won his war. In the same way, the only power the devil has on the battlefield is the power you give him by chomping on his bait of deception and getting hooked by his lies.

One teacher reminds us of this truth:

> The only power that Satan has is the power of deception, and the worst thing about deception is that you don't know you're being deceived. Otherwise, it wouldn't be deception. Once the truth is received, deception loses all its power. Therefore, Satan loses all his power when we know the truth.[3]

The truth is that God is in control and you are seated with Him in the heavenly order of spiritual authority. Remember the spiritual victory that was secured at the cross? The solid victory of the spiritual war is stated best in Colossians 2:15: "And having disarmed the powers and authorities, he made a public spectacle of them, triumphing over them by the cross."

When Jesus died, He disarmed the powers and authorities. Not only was the war won, but the rulers of darkness were disarmed. Their weapons were made null and void. The spiritual battles you fight today are fought with an enemy who has been defeated and disarmed. Neither Satan nor his demons have any authority or power over you if you have received God's gift of salvation and been born again.

It's almost embarrassing when I put it that way, isn't it?

Satan certainly doesn't *seem* to be as harmless as I've made him sound, but he is! Satan's power is no longer in actual weapons but in lies that he cons you into believing. He is an expert at exaggerating his lies and diminishing God's truth. Consider the thoughts that consume your attention. Which receive more mental energy, your problems or God's promises?

Choose to accept this truth: Christ's victory on the cross is your victory on the battlefield today. You don't really win anything now; you just appropriate the win that was accomplished on the cross when Jesus cried out, "It is finished!"

But how does that work, really? I'm glad you asked. In the rest of part 2, I'm going to revisit the three reasons we lose our battles and how we can counteract them.

Three Reasons We Lose Our Battles

Here are the three reasons we lose our battles today, as mentioned in chapter 4. Through the power of deception, Satan

1. Confuses you concerning your identity in Christ; we will discuss this in chapter 6.
2. Keeps you ignorant of how to exercise your spiritual authority; we will address this in chapters 7 and 8.
3. Hinders you from tapping into the "glorious riches of your spiritual inheritance" while you're fighting your battles; we will address this in chapters 9 and 10.

Is the Battle Really All in My Head?

Yes. And that is good news. If you're humble enough to admit it, you will soon discover that Satan is nothing more than a big mouth. As you learn to expose him to the light, you will see that he and his demons scatter like cockroaches.

QUESTIONS TO CONSIDER

1. How does the Enemy use your past to haunt your present?
2. What lies have you believed concerning your favored position in Christ?
3. What power does Satan have over you?

6

You Are a Child of God!

Scripture teaches us that we have victory over the Enemy because we are "alive in Christ" (Ephesians 2:5 MSG). Our lives "in Christ" share the victory that Jesus won at the cross. But until we understand what this means, Satan takes full advantage of our ignorance and smacks us about on the battlefield. Don't you want to know what it means to be "alive in Christ"?

Second Corinthians 5:17 says this: "Therefore, if anyone is in Christ, *the new creation has come*: The old has gone, the new is here!" (emphasis mine).

When I invited Jesus into my heart, I was mostly focused on heaven and hell. I was eleven, and I preferred heaven over hell, and life to death. I didn't think much about resurrection power or victory over darkness or freedom from bondage. I kind of thought that once I was baptized I was good to go; I'd surrendered my life to Christ, accepted His forgiveness for my sins, invited Jesus into my heart, and understood that I'd go to heaven when I died. Yes, He was Lord, but that was a given. Who wouldn't make the Savior

Lord? Why not? He might as well be in charge of my life. I didn't have a clue what to do.

But now that I've lived another forty plus years on earth, I've come to understand that Jesus' involvement in my life is just as much for the here and now as it is for the sweet by and by. I agree with my friend Jennifer Kennedy Dean that Jesus is not a vapor-like spirit who comes into my heart to sort of waft gently in a corner and wait to be summoned for help when things get scary. He's pushy and assertive. He comes in to take over, and He doesn't hesitate to make His presence known.

I've learned that making Him Lord is a daily thing, and that there's quite a tussle sometimes between Him and me. "Who's going to be in charge today?" has become a day-by-day quiet time consideration. I've bowed down to His rule in my life long enough to discover the incredible adventure of joining His cause. And I've also come to see that He told us the truth every step of the way. The biggest truth being that I can do absolutely nothing apart from Him (John 15:5).

When I said yes to Jesus at eleven, I had no idea where I was headed. It was much the same as when I said yes to Tom McCoy when I was twenty-three. I don't regret either decision, and am eager to be a better partner in both relationships. Today, I read God's Word in wonder and am challenged by statements like these:

I can do all this through him who gives me strength.

Philippians 4:13

And my God will meet all your needs according to the riches of his glory in Christ Jesus.

Philippians 4:19

You, dear children, are from God and have overcome them, because the one who is in you is greater than the one who is in the world.

1 John 4:4

And we are confident that he hears us whenever we ask for anything that pleases him. And since we know he hears us when we make our requests, we also know that he will give us what we ask for.

1 John 5:14–15 NLT

I could keep on going, but you get the idea. Are there promises in the Bible that baffle you? Are there some that challenge you? Is there anything in there that seems to contradict what you're going through in your home? If you answered yes to any of those questions, you are confused over who you are in Christ. And at the source of your confusion is this tiny little *i*.

This Tiny Little *i* That Causes Such Trouble

My father is with me right now at my "laughing place" (an eighty-year-old farmhouse in the mountains of North Carolina, where I do most of my writing). He's a writer too. He writes mysteries. He told me today that he has an idea for a nonfiction book. He wants to title it *i*. He went on to say that his book would be about this tiny little letter that represents an enormous obstacle between us and the victory we have in Christ as we live out our faith on earth.

Oh, how right he is! There is this tiny little *i* that causes such trouble.

The way of the world is to exalt self above all else. It is the way of the world to look out for yourself, to protect yourself, to advance yourself, and to make a way for your . . . self.

Jesus' disciples were guilty of an "I" mentality. Do you recall how often they argued among themselves? More than once the Gospel writers record their arguing over who would be the greatest in the kingdom of God once Jesus secured His throne. James's and John's mother even got into the fight:

Then the mother of Zebedee's sons came to Jesus with her sons and, kneeling down, asked a favor of him.

"What is it you want?" he asked.

She said, "Grant that one of these two sons of mine may sit at your right and the other at your left in your kingdom."

"You don't know what you are asking," Jesus said to them. "Can you drink the cup I am going to drink?"

"We can," they answered.

Jesus said to them, "You will indeed drink from my cup, but to sit at my right or left is not for me to grant. These places belong to those for whom they have been prepared by my Father."

When the ten heard about this, they were indignant with the two brothers.

Matthew 20:20–24

Jesus' disciples were looking out for them*selves*. They had their minds rooted in the things of this world and the cares of this life. Jesus' disciples were doing what came naturally—they were posturing for position. It wasn't until after His death, resurrection, ascension back to heaven, and the descent of the Holy Spirit that His disciples no longer lived self-centered lives.

Satan's aim is to dethrone the Lord from His position of authority in the world today. Often he doesn't have to go any further than an appeal to your tiny little *i* to accomplish mutiny in your life. This is why Jesus gave an interesting recruitment speech.

Then he said to them all: "Whoever wants to be my disciple must deny themselves and take up their cross daily and follow me."

Luke 9:23

Until we take these words to heart, we will remain confused over who we are in Christ.

I wish Jesus had been speaking figuratively when He told His disciples to shoulder their crosses. But a short time later, He did just what He said we should do if we want to follow Him.

Jesus denied himself,

. . . took up His cross

. . . and followed His Father, whose will was for His Son to die a painful, agonizing death.

We love what Jesus did *for us,* but we don't think too much about what Jesus said we'd need to do to follow Him. We come into our faith with an I-centered mentality.

I want to go to heaven when *I* die.

I want to be forgiven of *my* sins.

I want to experience victory in *my* life.

I, me, my remind me of the birds in the movie about the little clown fish, *Finding Nemo:* "*Mine, mine, mine!*"

The first step to clearing up the confusion over who you are in Christ is to take to heart Luke 9:23 and deal with this tiny little *i* that causes such trouble.

You Must Be Born Again

In order to live our lives in Christ, we must deal with the tiny but ferocious *i,* and the best way to do that is to be born again.

When Jesus met Nicodemus, the Pharisee who came to him at night, Jesus told him that in order to enter the kingdom of God one must be born again. This expression baffled Nicodemus. He exclaimed, "How can I be born again? I can't reenter my mother's womb!" (see John 3:4).

No, you can't, Nicodemus. Jesus was talking figuratively this time and using the analogy of birth. Kingdom life is to the Christ follower what birth is to the human.

When did your life begin? The moment you were born, or some-time before that? I believe that life begins at the moment of conception, and I know that my children were living some nine months before they were born. My own body experienced the impact of their lives. And while God created my womb to be the perfect place for them, they outgrew that temporary home. The womb was perfect until it was time for them to leave it. When that time came, the once perfect environment for my baby became hostile. So hostile that if they'd refused to exit, they would have died. So with no small effort on my part, my babies were born.

But once they were born, they entered into a new world to experience a different kind of life. Everything changed! They ate differently, they slept differently, they moved differently, and all the stuff that sustained them in the womb was thrown away. My children's lives didn't actually *begin* on their birth date. On the day they were born their lives continued as they transitioned to a different world. They were birthed from my womb into life on earth. You could say they were born when they were conceived, and they were "born again" when they were birthed into this world.

Just the telling of this reminds me of the day I read a preschool-appropriate book to my son. The little picture book introduced small children to the wonder of life. On one page there were thousands of tiny dots with one tiny dot a different color than the others. The caption said something about how God created you inside your mother's body in a secret place where only He knew about you. The book went on to tell some pretty basic stuff about where babies come from. When I finished reading it, I asked my four-year-old son if he had any questions. He said, "Wow! That's cool. I was just thinking, it's really good that we don't come into the world when we're just a tiny dot. I bet our mothers and fathers would lose us!" He had a point there! And the truth is that God did create us and knit us together in our mother's womb. We lived in that place until we were big enough and ready to live in a different world.

Jesus was telling Nicodemus that *in this same way* life in the kingdom is different from life in this world. When we become Christ followers, our orientation to our new life in Christ is as different as that of a baby who goes from his mother's womb to her open arms. The more we learn about and practice the principles of the kingdom, the more we experience life that is ours in Christ.

In order to clear the confusion over who you are in Christ, take God at His Word. Trust His provision, bank on His promises, when in conflict defer to His plan, and gradually your life will begin to illustrate the truth of God's Word (including the statements in the verses mentioned earlier: Philippians 4:13, 19; 1 John 4:4; 5:14–15). You will be able to do all things through Christ who gives you strength. God will supply all that you need out of His glorious riches. You will overcome and you will be confident that whatever you ask in His name will be given to you.

Christ in You or You in Christ?

Part of the reason we struggle with understanding who we are *in Christ* is that we imagine Christ being *in us*. We invite Jesus into our lives rather than our entering into His.

Well, isn't this just a play on words?

No, it isn't.

When I think of Jesus coming into my life, my life looms larger than Jesus, and He just comes in to straighten things out and assist me with living. I might never admit it, but deep down I think of Him as a friend and companion and a go-to power that I anxiously call on when I can't get what I want on my own or I'm in desperate need to get out of trouble.

When I think of myself entering into the life of Christ, suddenly my life takes on a whole new meaning. It's no longer about me. I'm not in control! I've entered into a world where what I want takes a backseat to what He wants. I didn't get Him, He got me. Why He wants me I don't know, for I can't be a go-to power for Him! And yet He wants me to be in His heart! He wants me for a friend and companion and a partner to accomplish His will on earth as it is in heaven. Of course, He doesn't expect me to bring anything to the table except my utter dependence on Him and absolute confidence in Him.

Is Christ in you, or are you in Christ? Consider an empty drinking glass and an aquarium filled with water.

- You could dip the glass in the water and you would have the water in the glass.

- Or, you could put the glass in the aquarium and you would have the glass in the water.
- Or, you could put the water in the glass and then put the glass in the aquarium and you would have the glass in the water and the water in the glass.

Which of these is the best description of your life in Christ?

I want mine to be the third description, I in Him and He in me, just like Jesus prayed in John 17: "I have given them the glory that you gave me, that they may be one as we are one—I in them and you in me—so that they may be brought to complete unity. Then the world will know that you sent me" (vv. 22–23).

I hope that you are settling any confusion you might have over who you are in Christ. For when you discover your proper position in God's heart, you will be able to battle boldly from that post. You are a born-again, new creation in Christ: "I have been crucified with Christ and I no longer live, but Christ lives in me. The life I now live in the body, I live by faith in the Son of God, who loved me and gave himself for me" (Galatians 2:20).

Greater Is He Who Is in You

The power that comes from knowing who you are in Christ is rooted in this truth recorded in 1 John 4:4: "You, dear children, are from God and have overcome them, because the one who is in you is greater than the one who is in the world."

Once you understand that you are in Christ and Christ is in you, His victory is your victory and you fight with the full authority of Christ. We will discuss exactly what that means in the next chapter.

If Anyone Is in Christ, Is He Really a New Creature?

Yes! In Christ you are no longer a slave to the things of this world. As you learn to think like a child of God, you will realize that because of your position in Christ, you have authority over the prince of this present darkness.

"If anyone is in Christ, the new creation has come: The old has gone, the new is here!" (2 Corinthians 5:17).

QUESTIONS TO CONSIDER

1. What compelled you most when you accepted Jesus' gift of salvation?
2. What does it mean to be born again?
3. How do you think about your relationship with Christ? Do you think in terms of Christ being in you, or you being in Him, or both?

What on Earth Is Spiritual Authority?

A solid understanding of spiritual authority is absolutely necessary for winning spiritual battles in your home. We discussed spiritual authority briefly in chapter 3, but we are going to dive deeper into that discussion here. What is spiritual authority? Spiritual authority is the right to rule the heavenlies (which in turn rule the earth), and this right belongs to God.

He is the one and only Supreme Ruler of the universe.

There are no other gods.

God's Supreme Power

All other gods are various manifestations of demons, or figments of human imagination, and therefore subject to the victory of the cross. Spiritual authority is the exercise of God's perfect will over all creation from beginning to end.

God's supreme power was never in question. He didn't gain back through the cross power lost when Adam and Eve ate the forbidden fruit. Even before Jesus' death on the cross, God had all authority in heaven and on earth. He demonstrated this authority when He flooded the earth, when He delivered Isaac to Abraham and Sarah in their old age, when He put Joseph in the seat of power in Egypt, when He brought the plagues against the Egyptians and set His people free, when He led them through the wilderness and gave them victory when they took possession of the Promised Land. The Old Testament is filled with one account after another illustrating the supreme power, wisdom, rule, and reign of God.

Jesus Exercised Spiritual Authority

When Jesus came to earth, He continued to exercise spiritual authority throughout His earthly ministry. In fact, the exercise of this authority was one of the aspects of His teaching that set Him apart from others: "The people were amazed at His teaching, because he taught them as one who had authority, not as the teachers of the law" (Mark 1:22).

When Jesus died, He redeemed mankind. Through His unfaltering obedience to God, Jesus fulfilled God's purpose (to a T), and released us from Satan's power. Then, when he rose from the dead, Jesus commissioned us with the assurance that we could now have the same authority that was His (the Great Commission, Matthew 28:18–20). Today, Jesus continues to exercise spiritual authority from His position at the right hand of God: "Now Christ has gone to heaven. He is seated in the place of honor next to God, and all the angels and authorities and powers accept his authority" (1 Peter 3:22 NLT).

Note that angels, authorities, and powers are subject to Christ. All spiritual powers are subject to Christ, who rules over them from the right hand of God. Spiritual authority belongs to God; it always has and it always will. Satan led a rebellion against God's authority and was soundly defeated (see Isaiah 14:12–15; Revelation 12:7–9). He and the third of heaven's army that followed him in the rebellion were cast down out of heaven. So where do they live now? Satan and his rebel angels, demons, reside in "the kingdom of the air" (Ephesians 2:2). I'm not exactly sure what this refers to—but I imagine it to be all around us. They also roam on the earth (Job 1:7; 1 Peter 5:8). From where demons dwell, they have access to us and their reality impacts ours.

The spiritual "power" of people who are not born again is limited to the earthly realm. They cannot rise higher than any other spiritual powers that hover in the "air." In *Spiritual Warfare for Women* I discuss the extent and limitations of the power of Satan and his demons by contrasting their fallen nature with God's original design. The Bible has a lot to say about angels, and a study of angels will give you insight into both the heavenlies and the realities of spiritual power.

For a simple illustration, imagine life on earth, life in the "air," and life with God in the highest heavens as spheres. Life on earth is our here and now. Surrounding the earth there is another sphere that I am calling the "air." Surrounding that sphere of "air" is another sphere that represents the highest heavens, where God sits on His throne. Each sphere's power is greater than the sphere before it. The authority to exercise that power is also greater than the one before. A person without Christ is also without hope, for he or she dwells in the sphere with the most limited power. Apart from Christ people are at the mercy of the powers of darkness, or the spirits of the "air." Satan, who dwells in the "air," gained power over the earth through the fall of man. Satan and his demons had nothing to rule over until Adam and Eve were created. But even though Satan gained the power of death as a result of sin, God always dwelt supreme over all of His creation! The reason God continues to engage in life on earth is because of His love for mankind, not because of a power struggle.

The power of sin that separated mankind from God was destroyed when Jesus died on the cross and God raised Him from the dead. Jesus came from the right hand of God in heaven; He penetrated the "air" (where heavenly beings exist) and lived on earth. He lived without sin, was crucified to pay for our sins, then resurrected from the dead, paving a way for mankind to be raised up with Him into the highest heaven. In Christ, we have power over principalities that exist in the "air." We have access to heaven's power and authority, which rule over the "air" and the earth. Here is my illustration of this truth:

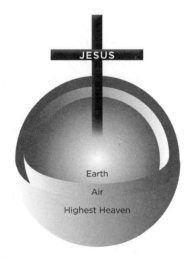

This is what I see: Through the cross of Christ we come to an intimate personal relationship with God. And with that intimacy we have access to His unmatched, unsurpassed power that is greater than the laws of nature and the laws of the principalities of darkness that swirl about in the "air." God allows His power to flow through us when we walk in oneness with Him. Our goal is to walk out the personal reality of Jesus' statement when He said, "I tell you the truth, anyone who believes in me will do the same works I have done, and even greater works, because I am going to be with the Father" (John 14:12 NLT).

The Enemy Has Been Defeated, Disarmed, and Made a Public Spectacle

This is a good place to be reminded of Colossians 2:15 and what I said earlier related to it. The Enemy has been *utterly defeated and completely disarmed*: "And having disarmed the powers and authorities, he made a public spectacle of them, triumphing over them by the cross."

In the days of Roman rule, when the New Testament was written, Rome's defeated enemy leaders were humiliated by being dragged through the streets of Rome in triumphal processions. Floats were built and pulled through the streets to reenact highlights of the battle. At the end of these parades, the crushed people were forced to walk amid the jeering crowds gathered to make a spectacle of them and their defeat. Then, following the captives, the conquered ruler was led by chains, sometimes maimed by the removal of their thumbs and toes. This represented their complete defeat and the fact that they would never hold a sword in battle or be able to stand erect.

After the Jews were defeated in AD 70, their leader, Simon, son of Giovas, was led through the streets of Rome in the victory parade with his head in a noose. When he arrived at the Forum, he was executed. After his execution, a cry of victory rang out through the people and they celebrated the defeat of their enemy.[1]

Tom and I walked in Simon's footsteps as we toured the Roman Forum with our travel guide. I can visualize these victory parades, and so could the Christians in Colossae. The early church believers in Colossae completely understood what Paul meant when he said that Jesus, "having disarmed the powers and authorities, made a public spectacle of them."

Jesus soundly defeated Satan on the cross. He disarmed him and made a public spectacle of him. I like to think of the diamond-studded sterling silver and gold crosses we wear as part of that ongoing triumphal parade. Satan used one of the cruelest forms of punishment this world has ever known to kill Jesus, and we wear those crosses as jewelry because God transformed what was evil into good.

Spiritual Authority in Your Home

God established spiritual authority in the heavenlies, but He also established it on the earth. One area of spiritual authority is in civil government (Romans 13). In Colossians 3:22–24, we are instructed to willingly submit ourselves to human government, as unto the Lord, when their laws do not contradict the laws of God.

Another area of spiritual authority is in the home. God ordered the home for effectiveness and efficiency. Husbands are to be the head of the household and wives are to give themselves to their leadership to demonstrate the role of the church in relationship to Christ (Ephesians 5). And children are to submit to their parents and grow to adulthood under the covering of their protection (Ephesians 6:1; Colossians 3:20).

We tend to think of authority as something to conquer rather than something to be embraced. This is because of the root of sin that continues to have power within us. When we deny our flesh, we release ourselves from the powerful cravings that tie us to the world. As we are released from the pull of the world, we begin to comprehend the realities and the truths that rule in the heavenlies. When we embrace these truths and strive toward one-ness with God, we execute the spiritual authority that is ours in Christ. If you want to experience the power of heaven, humble yourself under the mighty hand of God that he may lift you up in due time (1 Peter 5:6).

God is orderly. Spiritual power is executed in strict adherence to the law and order of God. You will begin to experience spiritual power when you embrace spiritual authority and choose to bow down under it. When your family functions in the proper spiritual order, your marriage and your children thrive. Husbands, you have great power before the throne of God when you pray for your wife and children, for you represent the head of your household. Wives, you also have great power in your home to release the power of God as you willingly yield to your husband's leadership. Children learn to embrace or reject authority by the example their parents set.

What on Earth Is Spiritual Authority?

Spiritual authority is the right to rule the heavenlies (which in turn rule the earth), and this right belongs to God. Spiritual authority becomes ours when we live in oneness with God. I will tell you more about how that works in the next chapter.

QUESTIONS TO CONSIDER

1. How does knowing that God is the only true God impact the way you approach your battles?
2. What comes to mind when you read Colossians 2:15?
3. Discuss what spiritual authority in your home means to you.

8

How Do We Exercise Spiritual Authority?

In preparation for what I'm about to write, I've read some crazy stuff. Some have said that we must speak aloud to the demons lurking in our lives and take full authority over them, casting them away. Others declare that we are tormented by territorial powers and that we must walk about and claim those territories for God in Jesus' name, singing praises, and therefore causing the powers of darkness to scatter. I read of attacks and torment and many terrible things.

And then I considered this: Jesus told us to exercise spiritual authority on earth. Then He showed us *how to exercise spiritual authority*. Why not let the author and finisher of our faith teach us how to exercise spiritual authority in our lives today? (Hebrews 12:1–2).

Step 1: Deny Yourself, Take Up Your Cross, and Follow Me

Let's go back to Luke 9:23. To exercise spiritual authority, you must first remove self from the throne of your life. Self-denial is absolutely essential. If you want to be a powerful force on the battlefield, you will learn to pray like Jesus: "Not my will, but yours be done" (Luke 22:42).

I mentioned this critical point earlier and said I would return to it. Here we are. At the end of chapter 2, I quoted a prayer that Richard Foster wrote, called the prayer of relinquishment. Let's talk about that prayer a bit more. Richard Foster describes the prayer of relinquishment like this:

> As we are learning to pray, we discover an interesting progression. In the beginning, our will is in struggle with God's will. We beg. We pout. We demand. We expect God to perform like a magician or shower us with blessings like Father Christmas. We major in instant solutions and manipulative prayers. In time, however, we begin to enter into a grace-filled releasing of our will and a flowing into the will of the Father. It is the prayer of relinquishment that moves us from the struggling to the releasing.[1]

When I was dealing with infertility (many years ago), I finally came to a place where I relinquished my desire for a baby. To be quite honest, I was tired of begging, and I hadn't found a way to convince Him that my ideas were better than His. So out of frustration and brokenness, I prayed. I told the Lord, "With or without a baby, I will serve you."

Immediately I felt a burden lifted. Where I had been whining and begging and confessing and professing, I was finally at peace. I mentioned the peace and joy that followed my prayer of relinquishment (I didn't know it had a name back then) to my sister Sharon while we were together at a retreat in Gatlinburg. I'll never forget our conversation.

"Sharon, I've finally surrendered to God. I've given Him my desire to have a baby. I am completely committed to serving Him with or without children. I've decided even to live the rest of my days with this deep longing in my heart if that's what He expects of me. Perhaps this is my ministry, to help women recognize that

God is worthy to be served even when and if He never answers our heart cries."

Sharon responded, "Well, I think it's great that you've surrendered, but I think it just stinks if God doesn't give you a baby. What kind of ministry is that, to go all around the world telling people God doesn't answer their prayers? I'd rather He honor your surrender and answer your prayer."

Secretly, I liked her response! But spiritually, I knew that when I surrendered, I surrendered it all. I gave God my good desires and trusted Him to replace them with His. Sometimes that's all God requires. In His relentless pursuit to develop the mind of Christ in you, sometimes He allows you to struggle until you surrender, and then He grants your request.

I prayed that prayer in April after three years of working hard to conceive, and in July I discovered I was pregnant. God gave me exceedingly abundantly more than I could ask or imagine, with three healthy babies in three years and then eighteen and twenty-two years later, He added two granddaughters before I knew I needed them!

But God doesn't always do that. A few years ago, my mother struggled to surrender my sister to the Lord, and after a long, hard, and precious battle with cancer, God took her. Sharon died while I was writing this manuscript.

These prayers of relinquishment are really "crucifixion moments." When you crucify your desires on the altar of God's will, you prove that you trust Him. You have to trust God in order to receive anything from Him. Often your own lack of trust binds the hands of God. His heart is willing, but His hands are hindered because you come before Him with an agenda of your own. In John 5:19 and 30, Jesus said that He could do nothing on His own. He came to do His Father's will. The prayer of relinquishment opens heaven's doors. You exercise spiritual authority when you pray this prayer.

Here is how *you* can pray the prayer of relinquishment.

Confess Your Worst Fear, Then Focus on God, Not You

Catherine Marshall wrote,

Fear is like a screen erected between us and God, so that his power cannot get through to us. So, how does one get rid of fear?

This is not easy when what we want most is involved. At such times, every emotion, every passion, is tied up in the dread that what we fear is about to come upon us. Obviously, only drastic measures can deal with such a gigantic fear and the demanding spirit that usually goes along with it. Trying to deal with it by repeating faith affirmations is not drastic enough.

So, then we are squarely up against the Law of Relinquishment. . . . In God's eyes, fear is evil because it's an acting out of a lack of trust in him.

Jesus is saying, admit the possibility of what you fear most. Force yourself to walk up to the fear, look it full in the face—never forgetting that God and his power are still the supreme reality—and the fear evaporates. Drastic? Yes. But it is one sure way of releasing prayer power into human affairs.[2]

I've allowed a reasonable fear to hinder me for quite some time. I gave everything else on my battlefield to God except the one thing that was captivated by my fear. For a while I thought my almost-absolute surrender was good enough—after all, even God must understand my reluctance to let go of this fear. But just this week I realized that partial surrender is not surrender at all. In order to experience the power that comes from heaven when you offer the prayer of relinquishment, you must relinquish it all.

Once I realized that my fear was evil because it was an "acting out" of my lack of trust in God, I let it go. I looked my fear full in the face, confessed it to God, and chose to trust His character and His love over my façade of protective control.

Now that I'm on the other side, I am asking myself, "What was I thinking, that I could do better than He could?" What do you fear? Admit the possibility of what you fear most; look it full in the face, remembering God is still in control. Then take whatever it is your fear held captive and give it to God.

Look full in His beautiful face, and when He whispers, "Do you trust me?" say, "I do."

Accept What Is With the Confidence That God Is Able to Change It at Any Time

Catherine Marshall also wrote this in reference to Jesus' prayer of relinquishment:

> "Dear Father . . . all things are possible to you. Please—let me not have to drink this cup! Yet it is not what I want but what you want" [Mark 14:36 PHILLIPS].
>
> The prayer was not answered as the human Jesus wished. Yet power has been flowing from his cross ever since.
>
> Even when Christ was bowing to the possibility of death by crucifixion, he never forgot either the presence or the power of God. The Prayer of Relinquishment must not be interpreted negatively. It does not let us lie down in the dust of a godless universe and steel ourselves for the worst.
>
> Rather it says, "This is my situation at the moment. I'll face the reality of it. But I'll also accept willingly whatever a loving Father sends."
>
> Acceptance, therefore, never slams the door on hope.[3]

But acceptance is equally never demanding of a holy, perfect, and righteous heavenly Father. Acceptance keeps you connected with God in spite of what His wisdom and love have allowed in your life.

As my mother took Sharon to her doctor's appointments, chemo treatments, scopes, and scans, she told me that she was trusting God. Many times my mother said, "Leighann, if I'm trusting Him at all, I have to trust Him with all. Otherwise, I'm not trusting Him." In all things we accept God's gifts in hope and submission.

And then to quote Richard Foster again,

The prayer of relinquishment is a bona fide letting go, but it is [also] a release with hope. We have no fatalist resignation. We are buoyed up by a confident trust in the character of God. Even when all we see are the tangled threads on the backside of life's tapestry, we know that God is good and is out to do us good always. That gives us hope to believe that we are the winners regardless of what we are being called upon to relinquish. God is inviting us deeper in and higher up. There is training in righteousness, transforming power, new joys, deeper intimacy.

Sometimes the very thing we relinquish is given back to us. This does not always happen, of course. There are times when the release is permanent. At such times we are to trust in the wisdom of God and ask for the grace to rest in His peace. A settled peace, in fact, is the most frequent experience of those who have trod the path of relinquishment.[4]

I am treading this peaceful path as I await God's answer to my heart cry. My mother is treading this peaceful path as she is sadly accepting His answer to hers. You can tread this path too. Face your fear and accept your reality, knowing that on the other side of crucifixion there is resurrection.

Give Up Your Will Completely

You can only give up your will completely when you consider your answers to these questions:

- Why should I doubt the goodness of God?
- Does God know best?
- Can I trust Him?

Ask yourself these questions, wrestle with their answers, and offer God a prayer of relinquishment. Then, see if you've finally let go. Here is how you can know if you've let go of your own will:

- You will start thanking God for the answer rather than begging Him to bring it.

- Your anxiety will be replaced by peace.
- You will carry inside you an expectant spirit rather than a desperate one.

You exercise spiritual authority when you deny yourself, take up your cross, and follow Him.

Step 2: Obey God's Word

Obedience is trust in action. Read God's Word and obey it. Obey Him when you don't understand Him. Obey Him when your heart is breaking. Obey Him when you long for Him to come to your rescue and yet see no help in sight. Obey God when you've surrendered your all and you're waiting for Him to respond.

Jesus said,

> Whoever has my commands and keeps them is the one who loves me. The one who loves me will be loved by my Father, and I too will love them and show myself to them. . . . Anyone who loves me will obey my teaching. My Father will love them, and we will come to them and make our home with them.

> John 14:21, 23

Obedience is the litmus test of true discipleship. You'll know you're a true follower of Jesus by measuring your decisions, attitudes, and behavior against God's Word. The Bible offers clear, specific, and definitive instructions on life. When you choose obedience over manipulation or control, you will unleash spiritual authority on the field of war.

You exercise spiritual authority when you maintain strict order in your life and choose to obey God's Word. Obedience is not *needed* by God. He's in full control, and all glory belongs to Him whether or not you choose to obey Him. But obedience is the way to keep your communication with Him uncluttered by the devil's lies and deceit. Obedience is the way to open the floodgate of

God's authority and power so that you can witness its unstoppable current gush right through the millions of evil spirits that hover over earth, champing at the bit to get a chance to have at you. Disobedience separates you from God; obedience keeps you united with Him.

Step 3: Embrace Humility

After Jesus *told* us to exercise spiritual authority, He showed us *how* to exercise spiritual authority.

> You must have the same attitude that Christ Jesus had. Though he was God, he did not think of equality with God as something to cling to. Instead, he gave up his divine privileges; he took the humble position of a slave and was born as a human being. When he appeared in human form, he humbled himself in obedience to God and died a criminal's death on a cross.
>
> Therefore, God elevated him to the place of highest honor and gave him the name above all other names, that at the name of Jesus every knee should bow, in heaven and on earth and under the earth, and every tongue declare that Jesus Christ is Lord, to the glory of God the Father.
>
> Philippians 2:5–11 NLT

Are you ready for this? Jesus clothed himself with humility—*then* He defeated the devil, destroyed death, broke the chains of sin, and set sinners free. Jesus exercised spiritual authority by making himself "nothing." You win your battles when your attitude is the same as Christ's.

Ugh! Wouldn't you rather wave a magic wand? And do some hocus-pocus?

I would.

I want a potion—you know: two roly-polys, one earthworm, some dirt, and a gummy bear. Mix it all together and smear it on your kid's feet while he's sleeping. When he gets up in the morning, he'll shape up and fly right. I want a command with spiritual force! I want to declare those demons unwelcome in my home and cast them out! I would have even used some incense! But instead, I get this:

1. Deny yourself, take up your cross, and follow Jesus.
2. Obey God's Word.
3. Embrace humility.

I'd rather do a hundred crunches than have to give up those offenses. I want to rise up in power and open my mouth and watch my enemies scatter. But the Supreme Ruler of the universe says to sit down and be quiet. He says, "My power is made perfect in weakness" (2 Corinthians 12:9). When we willingly step aside from the flesh, stop trying to control circumstances, and instead carry out biblical orders and let the Enemy spit and spew, we will experience sound victory, and we will know the battles were won in the name of Jesus and by nothing other than the power in the blood of the Lamb.

How Do We Exercise Spiritual Authority in Our Lives?

Exercising spiritual authority is simple really, but certainly not easy.

If you begin with the dying, the rest will amazingly fall into place.

Spiritual authority belongs to God. It's His to give to whomever He pleases. He will release spiritual authority to you when you deny yourself, take up your cross, and follow Jesus. You access spiritual authority over the darkness when you live your life in obedience to the commands of Christ. You exercise spiritual authority that breaks bondages when you embrace humility and make yourself "nothing."

It's simple, it's doable.

And when you do these things, you will be amazed at how the demons scatter. Your very presence in your home will command their attention. You will whisper, "Be gone," and their torment will cease.

QUESTIONS TO CONSIDER

1. Who has spiritual authority?
2. What right do you have to exercise spiritual authority?
3. How do you exercise your God-given spiritual authority?
4. Did this chapter surprise you?

9

What's So Glorious About Those Spiritual Riches?

We've discussed much in these chapters, so let me remind you of where we started and where we're going. In chapter 4, I explained that there are three reasons we lose our battles:

1. We are confused as to who we are in Christ. (I addressed this in chapter 6.)
2. We are ignorant of how to exercise spiritual authority in our lives. (I explained spiritual authority in chapters 7 and 8.)
3. We don't tap into the glorious riches of our spiritual inheritance, as described in Ephesians 1, while we're going to war in the trenches. This is where we are now.

Glorious Riches in the Trenches

The third reason we lose our battles against a defeated and disarmed opponent is that we don't tap into the glorious riches that are ours while we're battling in the trenches. Our battles are not against the devil himself; they are against his attacks on our faith. If we tremble in the trenches, he knows we are dealing with some kind of doubt regarding God's willingness or ability to meet our every need. He hopes that we have believed his lie that we are cut off from our supply line.

A critical aspect of warfare is keeping the supply lines going. Defensively, an army must have good logistics in managing soldiers' basic needs and the necessary weapons for war. Offensively, an army might disrupt the supply line of its enemy. I found this interesting:

> Napoleon Bonaparte once said, "An army marches on its stomach." His army lost more soldiers because of spoiled food than from the battle. In 1795, Napoleon offered a prize of 12,000 francs to anyone who could devise a reliable method of food preservation for his army. This effort resulted in the first attempts to store food for extended periods of time in cans and ultimately led to modern food canning methods.[1]

Napoleon knew what we forget. The supply line must stay strong. Too many of us are ill-equipped for the battles we're fighting. And although our supply lines have not been broken and our food never spoils, we lose our battles because we fall prey to the Enemy's lies and live as spiritual paupers when in reality we are children of the King. The King always gives His children more than enough provision to succeed.

In this chapter, you are going to discover the glorious riches that are yours for the war. By the time you reach the end, you're going to wonder why you ever doubted your provisions in the first place and how to bank on the abundance of them from this moment on.

Philippians 4:19, a Bodacious Promise

> My God will meet all your needs according to the riches of his glory in Christ Jesus.

There you have it, a bodacious promise right out of God's Word. God will supply all that you need. And when He does, His resources don't even begin to be exhausted.

The problem is:

We don't know what we need.

We don't know how to access what we need.

We don't know how to use what we need in battle.

Let's address these problems one at a time.

We Don't Know What We Need

So many times the devil defeats us by convincing us that we need one thing when we really need another. I may think I need a cup of coffee when I really need an hour of prayer. But that's not the soul-wrenching, messy stuff.

I've shared this before, but this is a good place to share it again. Two weeks after our daughter graduated from high school, she left us to live with her boyfriend. Tom and I hit our knees, which by the way is the "forward march" posture for winning spiritual war. We begged God to bring her home, and we prayed, "Lord, whatever you do, don't let her be pregnant! In Jesus' name, don't let her have a baby with that man."

A few weeks after we'd begun to pray this way, we discovered she was pregnant. I just *knew* that the win in my war was for my daughter Mikel to come home and for there to never ever be any long-term connection to her high school boyfriend.

I just *knew* it!

Not only that, but the win in my war was for Mikel to get her rear in gear and get herself in college, where she had over $76,000 in scholarships waiting for her. There was no way on God's green earth that my child was supposed to be a mama at eighteen and miss the next stage of her life. I didn't raise her for this.

I thought when Mikel became pregnant the devil was hearing my prayers better than God. I even told my husband that we should stop praying in specifics because it seemed we were giving the devil ideas. I thought I needed my daughter back without any babies, when God knew I really needed that baby. Don't ever forget that the plans of the Lord will not be thwarted (Job 42:2).

Misty was born a few months later, and in the first year of her life she and I became the very best of friends. The relationship we share is . . .

I'm trying to find words to describe it and I can't! She's . . .

. . . well, she's just more than I could ask or imagine. Here's a picture of her tickling my toes when I was in the hospital recovering from the surgery where half of my liver was removed because of cancer.

Misty was God's idea not Satan's. Satan held a temporary victory in my home when he tricked me into believing that he had somehow wrecked my daughter's life and stolen her from God's capable, faithful, sovereign hands. Through this painful battle,

God taught me so many things, perhaps the greatest being that there are times when I don't have a clue what I really need.

Many of my prayers are out of kilter. I beg God to give me things that are not what I really need. When He doesn't do what I tell Him to do, I get angry and confused and all put out with the seeming victory that Satan's scored.

Sometimes I'm like James and John's mother asking for something I don't really want. (I referenced this request in chapter 6 in the discussion of the *I* mentality.) How often do we pray our children out of trouble or into pleasure or even to avoid the natural consequences of their poor decisions?

I think there are many times when God might address me like Nanny McPhee addressed Simon when she made sure he was ready to face the consequences of his decision no matter what they might be. "Leighann, are you sure this is what you want? Are you willing to face the consequences?" (*Nanny McPhee* was a 2005 British comedy film.) I'm grateful that God superimposes His will over mine rather than letting me talk Him into something that would result in disaster.

How Much More

We tend to cut off our own supply line when we ask for the wrong things and get duped into thinking we need one thing when really we need another. I love what Jesus taught us in Luke 11:11–13:

> Which of you fathers, if your son asks for a fish, will give him a snake instead? Or if he asks for an egg, will give him a scorpion? If you then, though you are evil, know how to give good gifts to your children, how much more will your Father in heaven give the Holy Spirit to those who ask him!

Notice that the implication is that an earthly father will never give his son something evil when he asks him for something good. And yet Jesus didn't say the father would actually give his son what he was asking for, He just implied that the father would give good gifts to his children. But the real message here is in these three words: *how much more.*

"*How much more* will your Father in heaven give . . ."

"*How much more* will your Father in heaven give the Holy Spirit . . ."

"*How much more* will your Father in heaven give the Holy Spirit to those who ask him!"

Jesus told those listening that when we ask Him for things that we think are good, when we ask Him for what we think we want, *how much more* will He answer our prayers with what we really need, with all that will continue to supply us with all that we need all of the time!

"How much more will your Father in heaven give the Holy Spirit to those who ask him!"

Why ask for the gifts that come from the Spirit of God when you can have the Spirit himself?

Even when you don't know what to ask for, Jesus knows what you need, and *how much more* is He ready to give the Holy Spirit.

Even when you don't know exactly what you need, trust that the Spirit does, and when you receive more of Him, you receive the discernment to know what to request.

More of the Holy Spirit Is What You Need in Your Home

I cannot tell you how many discussions my husband and I have had regarding what we need to restore our family to its former glory. Our hearts, like yours, yearn to have a home that is whole again. We want God to be glorified in the unity of our family. My daughter Kaleigh discovered this verse five years ago when she was praying us through the crisis we were facing that still remains as I'm writing this book: "'The glory of this present house will be greater than the glory of the former house,' says the Lord Almighty. 'And in this place I will grant peace,' declares the Lord Almighty" (Haggai 2:9).

What a tremendous promise!

Throughout our ordeal, we've discussed schemes and strategies. We've entertained possibilities and plans. We've talked at length about what we could've, should've, would've done had we known then what we know now. We've thoroughly talked about what we think we need and how we might go about getting it. But finally, a few months ago, when we realized that we were completely at the mercy of God, we gave up all that talking and began to pray for more of Him.

The Holy Spirit is what you need. And *how much more* will your heavenly Father give the Holy Spirit to those who ask Him! Perhaps He's banking on your persistence as He seemingly delays in answering your prayers.

What's So Glorious About Those Spiritual Riches?

They are delivered in a person, the person of God himself in the form of the Holy Spirit. He is what you need. In the next chapter, I will tell you how to access the riches of God and how to use them in battle.

QUESTIONS TO CONSIDER

1. Think about the situation you are fighting today. When is the last time you felt like the devil scored a win?

2. Which of your prayers are not being answered right now? What might God be up to? Don't forget that nothing is impossible for Him.

3. What do you need most on your battlefield today? Can the Holy Spirit deliver that?

10

How Do I Access the Glorious Riches of God?

Now that you know you can expect God to give you what you need when you need Him, let's address how to maintain ready access to His provisions so that you can use them in battle. We lose our battles because we don't know how to keep those riches coming. The devil cuts us off from our supply line by coercing us into believing we have to jump through hoops to pry open the reluctant hands of God.

You don't have to convince God to give you what He's eager to give!

Does that mean you'll always get what you ask for? No. I addressed that reality in the previous chapter.

Does that mean you'll always get what you want when you want it? No, He doesn't work that way either.

Does that mean you'll always get what you need when you need it?

You can, but whether or not you do is up to you. And that is where we're going with this chapter. I'm going to expose three lies the devil tells you regarding your access to your supply line and three truths that will destroy those lies each and every time. If you choose to believe the truth, you will tap into the glorious riches of God. If you choose to embrace the lie, you will not.

Lie #1: God's Got What You Need but He Doesn't Want to Share It With You

One of the most difficult battles I face is this one. I'll be praying for God to do what only He can do, and the devil will reason with me in my prayer. "That makes sense to me. What you are asking is certainly reasonable! Why wouldn't God give you that?" And then, when my prayer isn't answered, the devil comes back and says, "I wonder why God's not answering your prayer. What if He doesn't want you to have that? Why wouldn't He want you to have that?"

There is nothing more tragic than a follower of Christ who is uncertain of her Father's willingness to meet her every need. And yet this tragedy is played out in many of our lives daily. Deep at the root of our need to control the people and circumstances that are beyond our control is the deeply rooted belief that we can't depend on God's willingness to meet our every need according to His riches in glory.

God's Word is the antidote to Satan's lies. What does God's Word say about God's willingness to provide us with all that we need?

Of course we have Philippians 4:19: "My God shall meet all your needs according to the riches of his glory in Christ Jesus."

And then we also have Luke 12:24: "Consider the ravens: They do not sow or reap, they have no storeroom or barn; yet God feeds them. And how much more valuable you are than birds!"

And Matthew 7:11: "If you, then, though you are evil, know how to give good gifts to your children, how much more will your Father in heaven give good gifts to those who ask him!"

These verses are not meant to frustrate you. They are meant to sustain you as you wait on your Father to come through for you. Commit one of these verses to memory and hurl it at the devil the next time he challenges your confidence that God is more than willing to give you what you need when you need it.

The other day I was struggling to believe. The devil knew it and was right there to challenge my faith. I'd completely released my situation to the Lord about three months ago, and with that release I'd experienced almost three months of peace and confidence that manifested itself by choosing to look away from things that were going on in the right now (things that contradicted what God assured me He would conquer). I know now that I'd prayed the prayer of relinquishment.

But after several months, I started to obsess over the things that were going on and thinking through how I might respond to them. (Just code for how I could manipulate and maneuver to get the outcome I desired.)

I began to cry out to God and beg Him for some sign that He was aware of what we were going through. I was online looking for an illustration for the Bible study I teach on Wednesday nights, when I ran across a great blog post by Priscilla Shirer. It was a good word.[1] At the end of her blog post, Priscilla printed 1 Thessalonians 5:24: "Faithful is He who calls you, and He also will bring it to pass" (NASB).

I smiled. *That* was my good word from the Lord. The reminder of 1 Thessalonians 5:24 was the portion of God's glorious riches He saw fit to serve me that day.

The very next morning I was reading one of Andrew Murray's books on prayer, and at the end of the chapter I was reading, he quoted 1 Thessalonians 5:24: "Faithful is He who calls you, and He also will bring it to pass" (NASB).

A double portion! Either that, or God said, "I'll say it again so you can hear me, Leighann."

I smiled, for I knew God was speaking directly to me. He was reassuring me that He is able *and* willing to make good on promises He's made to me as I've prayed through my battlefield.

Lie #1: God's got what you need but He doesn't want to share it with you.

Truth #1: God's got what you need and He wants to share it with you.

Lie #2: God's Got What You Need But You're Not Good Enough to Receive It

The second lie is a tricky one. For there are truths you need to embrace and discipline you need to exercise in order to grow in your understanding of what it means to partner with God in winning the battles in your home. But the primary position in Christ related to the outpouring of His glorious riches is one of simply receiving.

God is the giver.

You are the receiver. And the only requirement for you to receive what God has to give is for you to need it.

The devil will try to convince you that you need to pray better or more often or more consistently. While all of these are good ideas and certainly things that we should do, they are not prerequisites to receiving God's blessings.

The devil will also beat you up with what you didn't do in the past and therefore persuade you that you disqualified yourself from receiving anything from God. Oh my goodness, does he have a heyday with that! My Papa Smith often said, "You can't live your life backwards." And he was absolutely right. What's done is done. Sure you made mistakes! You're human! But you cannot return to yesterday and have a do-over. Satan will camp you out on the island of regret and beat you to a pulp with a whip made of memories if you're not careful.

Don't allow it. Take your thoughts captive and make them bow down to the lordship of Christ (2 Corinthians 10:5). Here are some verses to choose to believe in order to get in your little boat and escape from the island of regret:

> Brothers and sisters, I do not consider myself yet to have taken hold of it. But one thing I do: Forgetting what is behind and straining

toward what is ahead, I press on toward the goal to win the prize for which God has called me heavenward in Christ Jesus.

Philippians 3:13–14

And we know that in all things God works for the good of those who love him, who have been called according to his purpose.

Romans 8:28

What, then, shall we say in response to these things? If God is for us, who can be against us? He who did not spare his own Son, but gave him up for us all—how will he not also, along with him, graciously give us all things?

Romans 8:31–32

There are plenty of other verses in the Bible that combat the lies of Satan. Read God's Word, hide His Word in your heart (memorize it), and let the Spirit of God call these truths to battle when the devil goes to meddling in your mind.

Lie #2: God's got what you need but you're not good enough to receive it.

Truth #2: God's got what you need and He's eager to give it to you. Your goodness is irrelevant.

Lie #3: God Doesn't Really Have What You Need After All

This is one of the most wicked lies in Satan's arsenal: "God doesn't really have what you need after all; the world does." This is one of the lies that Satan used against Jesus. Think of the audacity of the devil! He is so full of arrogance that he thought he could convince Jesus to choose the world over heaven.

The devil led him up to a high place and showed him in an instant all the kingdoms of the world. And he said to him, "I will give you all their authority and splendor; it has been given to me, and I can give it to anyone I want to. If you worship me, it will all be yours."

Jesus answered, "It is written: 'Worship the Lord your God and serve him only.'"

Luke 4:5–8

The devil tempted Jesus to exchange His love for His Father for possession of the earth. What madness. The devil attempted to get Jesus, the perfect Son of God, to bow to him. Of course Jesus didn't; He reminded Satan that He was commanded to worship and serve God only.

But what about us? Doesn't the devil convince us that the world can deliver what God cannot?

What does alcohol do for some? Dull the pain, rid them of inhibitions, give a little buzz?

What about marijuana? Cocaine? Or a new car?

They all deliver what their consumers think they need. What do sex outside of marriage and pornography do for people? The devil takes many of our appetites and satisfies them temporarily with the pseudo riches of this world that are really death in disguise.

How do we resist these battles? How do we teach our children to resist the temptations of the flesh?

Take God at His Word. Live a lifestyle that is different from that of the world. In contrast to the culture, you should be peculiar. If you are not, you haven't proven to anyone, most of all your children, that you are any different than the rest of the world.

I've become a student of my young adult children. They challenge me by questioning many of the truths that I hold dear. They are part of a generation that's begging us to *show* them what we believe. They want us to prove our faith with our actions, and they shout to us that our actions speak louder than our words.

When our children are young, we rear them in moral safety zones. They embrace our ways of thinking, our lifestyle choices, and our words, as gospel. But as they grow, they start thinking for themselves. They hear other ways of thinking, they discover other lifestyle choices, and they test the truths we've taught them.

This testing of truth is perfectly natural and actually healthy. As your children grow up, respect their freedom to make their own decisions. Let the natural consequences of poor choices play out in their lives. Live consistent with your words, and pray. Show your children that you trust God's provision for you. He's the only one who has what you need. Satan's got a lot of substitutes. They might seem good at first, but all of Satan's counterfeits lead to death. Don't fall for this lie.

Here are some verses that will go to combat against this lie.

And God is able to bless you abundantly, so that in all things at all times, having all that you need, you may abound in every good work.

2 Corinthians 9:8

So do not fear, for I am with you; do not be dismayed, for I am your God. I will strengthen you and help you; I will uphold you with my righteous right hand.

Isaiah 41:10

Every good and perfect gift is from above, coming down from the Father of the heavenly lights, who does not change like shifting shadows.

James 1:17

Lie #3: God doesn't really have what you need after all.
Truth #3: God, and only God, has what you need.

How Do I Access the Riches of God?

Reject the lies and embrace the truth.

1. God's got what you need and He wants to share it with you.
2. God's got what you need and He's eager to give it to you. Your goodness is irrelevant.
3. God, and only God, has what you need.

Take hold of God's promises and claim them as your own. All of God's promises are contained in His storehouse of glorious riches, and you can claim any or all of them at any or all of the time. There are over three thousand promises in God's Word, and He makes good on each one.

Read the Bible, invite God to speak to you as you read, and discover which of His promises He's serving to you today. I guarantee that He's got a promise for your battle, maybe several that you can cling to with all your might. And don't forget this great promise pertaining to all the others: "For no matter how many promises God has made, they are 'Yes' in Christ. And so through him the 'Amen' is spoken by us to the glory of God" (2 Corinthians 1:20).

QUESTIONS TO CONSIDER

1. Have you believed or are you now believing any of these lies? Which ones?
2. Read the "truth statements" in chapter 4 and be reminded that you are the beneficiary of all of God's spiritual riches!
3. Which promise of God is "Yes" for you today?

PART 3

What the Devil Doesn't Want You to Know

The nature of the enemy's warfare in your life is to cause you to become discouraged and to cast away your confidence. Not that you would necessarily discard your salvation, but you could give up your hope of God's deliverance. The enemy wants to numb you into a coping kind of Christianity that has given up hope of seeing God's resurrection power.

—Bob Sorge, *Glory: When Heaven Invades Earth*

11

The Devil Doesn't Want You to Know the Power of Love

I've already told you several things Satan doesn't want you to know, and I intend to tell you several more, but in these next few chapters there are three specific things I'm going to tell you that give you a definite advantage on the battlefield. These are truths that belong to you because you are in Christ. They are exclusive benefits for children of the King. These three things might seem to be so ordinary that you've taken them for granted. When I list them, you're going to sense a bit of disappointment, for you are most likely looking for something much more—how shall I say it—*supernatural*? But just like the truths I shared with you in regard to how to exercise spiritual authority, these are the *very* things Satan wants you to pass off as insignificant. He can't keep you from recognizing their reality, so he'll try to get you to dismiss their power.

Are you ready? Don't forget that we are addressing spiritual warfare for the family. Consider how these three truths affect your relationships with your spouse and your children. Think about the power they have to release the work of God in your home. Part of the training involved in becoming a great warrior is effectively developing the skill of connecting the promises of God with the circumstances in your life.

Here is the first of the three things the devil doesn't want you to know. It is the first of three superpowers that are rarely ever used effectively in battle:

You Are Loved; Therefore, You Can Love

Don't roll your eyes and flip through the pages, looking for what comes next! I told you these truths might sound trite. And if they do, it's only because Satan has done a phenomenal job of convincing you that they are void of power!

Have you ever thought about the most popular visual for angels? The devil has taken the truth about angels and recreated them to look like chubby little children with tiny little wings, flitting and floating about. If you'd been defeated by the most powerful warriors ever created, and you knew you were outnumbered by them two-to-one, wouldn't you want people to think of them as chubby little cherubs?

In the same way, the devil has distorted the power of love. In fact, this first truth might very well be the most powerful of all. *Love is a mighty force to be reckoned with.*

You Are Loved by God

You are loved! God chose you. He chose you because He's crazy about you! You are loved by God.

How cool is that?!

The God who created the world knit you together in your mother's womb and gave you the breath of life. He loved you so much that He chose to send His own Son to die on the cross so He could have a personal relationship with you.

Even if no one else were to love you, God chooses to love you. You are loved.

The fact that you are loved by the Supreme Power of the Universe is no small thing. The other morning I was driving to work when I was overwhelmed by the implications of this question/ declaration of faith: "If God is for us, who can be against us?" (Romans 8:31).

Think about that!

You might have a wealthy benefactor or a rich relative. I don't. Tom and I did, however, have a wealthy friend who anonymously paid for his seminary tuition. We knew who it was, but since he didn't want us to know, we pretended we didn't. We knew never to bank on his generosity, so we managed our finances so that we could pay tuition when it was due. But at the beginning of one semester the car needed major repairs and we didn't have enough money to pay for the car and for tuition. Tom went to the comptroller at the seminary to discuss a payment plan, and he discovered his bill was paid in full. Imagine our delight!

While we didn't want to presume upon our benefactor's generosity, God invites us to presume upon His love!

> What, then, shall we say in response to these things? If God is for us, who can be against us? He who did not spare his own Son, but gave him up for us all—how will he not also, along with him, graciously give us all things?
>
> Romans 8:31–32

The other morning, when this thought came to me, it struck me that I rarely ever tap into my heavenly benefactor's invitation to look to Him for my resources. I typically use my own feeble efforts to scrape together what I need from limited supplies.

You are loved by a generous God who has all that you need for all that you're going through all of the time (2 Corinthians 9:8).

Live like you know and believe it.

Because You Are Loved, You Can Love

Because you are loved, you can love.

You can love the way God loves.

Only those who have a personal relationship with God can love the way God loves.

Others cannot do it.

They may have pieces and reflections of pure love, but they can't love like God. Only God can love like God, and you can love like God when you allow His love to flow through you.

Scripture teaches us that "God is love" (1 John 4:8). God is not just the demonstrator of love; He *is* love. Love doesn't define God; God defines love. If you want to know what love is, study God. Those who know God know love and in the knowing comes the growing. Consider how love goes to war.

Love Goes to War

Love conquers all offenses. When quarrels break loose, love diffuses the emotion-charged atmosphere. When you respond to someone's outburst by turning the other cheek, you usher God onto the front line of your war. Many unnecessary arguments are avoided with love.

Proverbs 10:12 says, "Hatred stirs up quarrels, but love makes up for all offenses" (NLT).

Love covers a multitude of sins. Where sin gets the upper hand, love has the last word. When you choose love over revenge, or love rather than resentment, bitterness, or score-keeping, you leave room between yourself and the person who hurt you for God to do a great and mighty thing.

1 Peter 4:8 says, "Above all, love each other deeply, because love covers over a multitude of sins."

Love works (hard)! First Corinthians 13:4–8 describes the hard work of love:

Love is patient, love is kind. It does not envy, it does not boast, it is not proud. It does not dishonor others, it is not self-seeking, it is not easily angered, it keeps no record of wrongs. Love does not delight in evil but rejoices with the truth. It always protects, always trusts, always hopes, always perseveres. Love never fails.

This kind of hardworking love is powerful.

Love is doable.

Love is natural for a Spirit-filled follower of God.

Love in the Trenches of Battle

I was worshiping one Sunday morning with my arms raised high in praise to the Lord. I had my eyes closed, and I was thinking of how much I love the Lord. Out of nowhere I heard (a definitive thought came to my mind from God) a voice saying, "Leighann, what are you doing?" I quickly responded, "I'm worshiping you, Lord. Oh, how I love you this morning."

God responded, "No you're not, Leighann. You're not worshiping me."

I was not surprised; I knew exactly where He was going with this. "I am, Lord. I'm worshiping you."

"You can't worship me and harbor hatred for one I love." I knew precisely who He was talking about.

"Lord, you know that I can't love him right now. He's . . ." And I proceeded to tell God of all the ways he'd offended me and wounded me deeply. Of course God knew all of this already, but I felt like He needed to be reminded.

"I'm not interested in all of that. I want you to know that when Jesus hung on the cross, you and [that man] were standing on level ground. You weren't on a little rise that brought you closer to the flow. You were both right there, guilty, helpless, in desperate need of a Savior."

I was broken. "Lord, you know that you are asking me to do something that I simply cannot do."

He had a ready response: "Leighann, I don't expect you to love him. I love him already. I am asking you to yield to me and let the love I have for him flow from me through you."

I was relieved. I was off the hook! I didn't have to muster up love in me to please God. All I had to do was bow down to Him and let His love rule in my life. I knew how to do that. I knew how to yield to God. I've had lots of practice submitting to the lordship of Christ in my life—since I was eleven.

When I love the lovable, I'm only as good as the worst criminal. My husband often says, "Even the Mafia loves their own children!" But when I love the unlovable, the undeserving, the ones who've injured me most, *then* I'm demonstrating to the world the love of God. That kind of love moves mountains, wins wars, and establishes God's kingdom on earth as it is in heaven.

Let Love Rule in Your Home

When a country is at war, there is no peace in the streets. Curfews are set, rights of the citizens are denied, and fear rules. If you're not careful, spiritual battles in your home can result in the same warlike atmosphere. In a home where fear rules parents execute their own "martial law." Martial law in a spiritual war-zone home might include these restrictions:

1. Boundaries are tightened and strictly enforced.
2. Secrets are expected to be kept.
3. A zero tolerance rule might be put into effect.

Boundaries are tightened and strictly enforced. I know parents who punish law-abiding children for the offenses of the one child who broke the law. They are so afraid of what might happen to their other children that they impose stricter boundaries on them. I know a family that never let their daughter spend the night with friends or have friends over to spend the night at their house because of the shenanigans of an older sibling. The younger sister suffered more restrictions in her home because her parents feared that without them she might end up like her older sister.

What does the superpower of love look like in your home? When you release love in your home, you kill fear—with a solemn understanding of the sovereignty of love.

You practice your faith. Did you catch that word *practice*? Faith that faces fear is faith that does something. When you exercise faith, you refuse to react to circumstances that are beyond your control. You don't change your entire parenting style simply because one child made poor choices. You stay the course, and you trust God.

Secrets are expected to be kept. Where battles rage, children quickly learn that some subjects are taboo. Even small children will learn to keep quiet about their parents' arguments, Dad's drinking, or their older siblings' disrespect for their parents. They know the behavior isn't right, but they also feel the burden of keeping it secret. They know innately that those conflicts are off-limits in conversations with others. People who live in battle zones become experts in covert operations. They learn to keep their secrets hidden and to "put on a happy face" for those outside their home.

When you learn to execute the superpower of love, you don't let secrets fester in your family. You refuse to be afraid of what others might think.

My husband and I both speak publicly in ministry. We've determined to never live a private life that is in conflict with our public life. In fact, we open the windows and the doors to our lives and speak out about what we have going on. When our children were young, Tom gave them one dollar for every reference they heard him make to them in his sermons. The only time we ever hid anything from the public was in the four weeks following our teenage daughter's decision to leave our home and move into an apartment with her boyfriend. We were so devastated by her move that we didn't know exactly what we should do where our "public" was concerned. After much prayer and consultation with our partners in ministry, we decided to be forthright and honest with our congregation. On a Sunday morning we stood together and told the church what was happening in our home.

Suspicions, half-truths, and rumors were already rampant during the four weeks of our silence. By opening up our broken hearts, we took the power out of the shadows. Satan dwells in the darkness, and truth always sheds light on the darkness. Fear causes us to want to hide in the shadows. But perfect love casts out fear.

A zero tolerance rule might be put into effect. When fear rules, some people put up last-ditch efforts to regain control. Parents who sense they are losing their children to bad company might try to impose their authority and forbid a child to hang out with those friends. Their discussions over the situation might be one-sided, with Dad doing most of the talking, Mom crying, and the son or daughter trying desperately to be heard. Impenetrable walls spring up between parent and child or even between husband and wife, or both, and the devil has a heyday.

As you develop your superpower love skills, you will learn to disengage from the invitation to go toe-to-toe with an angry spouse or child. I have a friend who gives wise counsel to many people. We've learned to honor him like a prophet. He told one of my prayer partners today to "stop getting in the ring with the devil." He went on to say, "That's not your fight." He was referencing her tendency to be drawn into a combat zone with a family member who is temporarily blind to what is right and what is wrong. The devil loves to woo us into hand-to-hand combat where we try to convince a lost loved one of their lostness. We can't win the war that way.

Love Is Long-Suffering

Love allows a mom to turn the other cheek when her son lashes out at her for daring to challenge his toxic relationship with his girlfriend. Love shuts a father's mouth and drives him to his knees when his daughter continually takes his generosity for granted while insisting on continuing her addiction.

Love knows there is power in silence.

Love listens when she needs to talk, even when she's off base and terribly mistaken.

Love embraces him, and his significant other, even when that other is also male.

Love never stands on a soapbox and shouts.

Love loses sleep, cries out to God in prayer, and lies on the floor with her while she weeps.

Love never gives up.

One of the most beautiful examples of love was shown us in the life of Elisabeth Elliot, who returned to share the love of Christ with the Auca Indians after they killed her husband. She personified 1 Corinthians 13:4–8:

> This love of which I speak is slow to lose patience—it looks for a way of being constructive. It is not possessive: it is neither anxious to impress nor does it cherish inflated ideas of its own importance.
>
> Love has good manners and does not pursue selfish advantage. It is not touchy. It does not keep account of evil or gloat over the wickedness of other people. On the contrary, it is glad with all good men when truth prevails.
>
> Love knows no limit to its endurance, no end to its trust, no fading of its hope; it can outlast anything. It is, in fact, the one thing that still stands when all else has fallen.
>
> PHILLIPS

You are loved; therefore, you can love. Don't let the devil tell you that your love is weak. The love of God saved your soul while it defeated Satan. The love of God flowing through you to others will continue to save souls, change the world, and bring victory to the war waging in your home.

QUESTIONS TO CONSIDER

1. What does it mean to be loved by God?
2. Who do you need to love like Jesus loved you?
3. What might the power of love do in your home?

12

The Devil Doesn't Want You to Know the Power of Forgiveness

The second truth the devil doesn't want you to know is this:

You Are Forgiven; Therefore, You Can Forgive

Yeah, you didn't see that one coming, did you?

Here it is, the second of three truths the devil wants you to dismiss: the power of forgiveness.

Okay, hear me out. I'll go ahead and confess that I don't want to write this chapter. I'm much better at baptizing my unforgiveness than I am at letting offenses go. I'm really good at bringing up the past at the most opportune moments to make valid points in strategic arguments. I've even been known to find ways to use past offenses as message illustrations. Thank goodness the people who've offended me don't search out and listen to my messages on the Internet!

I'm not so good at forgiveness. Nevertheless, truth is powerful, and if I want to obey God, I will present this truth to you even when it means I will have to apply it to my own corner of the battlefield. So here we go . . .

Deep breath, whispered prayer, let's do this thing.

Forgiveness is a common grace. As human beings, even apart from a personal relationship with God, we know that we should forgive. Most world religions teach forgiveness as a core value. But for the follower of Christ, forgiveness is at the very heart of our faith. We are never more like Christ than when we forgive those who've mistreated us, wounded us, crippled us, or violated our rights.

Jesus commanded us to forgive when He taught us to pray, warning us that if we didn't forgive others, God wouldn't forgive us (Matthew 6:12–15). He also showed us how to forgive when He hung on the cross and cried out, "Father, forgive them, for they do not know what they are doing" (Luke 23:34).

Not only are we never more like Christ than when we forgive, but we are also never more vulnerable to the Enemy's deceptive power than when we choose not to forgive. And this, my friend, is why this weapon is so powerful. When you exercise your ability to forgive, you disarm your enemy.

Forgiveness Defined

Before I explain the power of forgiveness, let's define forgiveness.

> **Forgiveness** is the intentional and voluntary process by which a victim undergoes a change in feelings and attitude regarding an offense, lets go of negative emotions such as vengefulness, with an increased ability to wish the offender well.[1]

I thought that was an interesting definition, especially coming from Wikipedia.

Here's another definition from biblical counselor June Hunt:

Forgiveness is dismissing your demand that others owe you something, especially when they fail to meet your expectations, fail to keep a promise, and fail to treat you justly.[2]

And here's a great definition from talk show host Oprah Winfrey, who condensed what one of her guests said on the show:

Forgiveness is giving up the hope that the past could be any different.[3]

These are all great definitions of forgiveness. But the best definitions are those that are illustrated for us through real life. When my children were preschoolers, I left my full-time job as a consultant in our denomination's state convention to stay home with them. During that time, I wrote curriculum for children's missions organizations as both a hobby and a little bit of supplemental family income. My assignments put me in touch with men and women who were taking the gospel to the uttermost parts of the earth.

One month's unit was focused on the country of Rwanda. In 1994, one of the most horrific genocides took place in Rwanda when the Hutu tribe systematically slaughtered as many as 75 percent of the Tutsi tribe. An estimated one million people were killed in three months while the international community watched.

I was given the name of a missionary serving in Rwanda who had lived through the nightmare of this genocide. This was before the remarkable invention of the Internet, so I conducted interviews by airmailing questions, along with blank cassette tapes, to my contacts. They recorded their answers on the cassettes and mailed them back to me. The Rwandan missionary I interviewed was a medical doctor. He literally wept as he answered my questions. He recounted story after story of the senseless killing that descended on his village. Neighbors killed neighbors, church members killed church members. He told of rapes, fires, and merciless murders of men, women, and children, mostly by machete. I was writing for children, so I couldn't say as much as I wanted to when I delivered the Rwandan unit for publication. But I will never forget that doctor's tears as he relived the horrors on the cassette tape interview.

I discovered one of many remarkable stories of forgiveness that came out of the Rwandan genocide. Immaculée Ilibagiza (a Tutsi) was a young university student when she hid in the bathroom of a Hutu minister's house with seven other Tutsi women to escape certain death. As the Hutus carried out their brutal murders just outside the tiny bathroom window, these women huddled together in fear. In her book *Left to Tell*, Immaculée recounts her terror and her understandable anger toward the senseless violence that left all of her family dead. She confessed on the CBS morning show that although she prayed the Lord's Prayer over and over again, she could not repeat the words "forgive us our trespasses as we forgive those who trespass against us."

Who could blame her?

But, in that bathroom, where she hid for three months and wasted away from 115 to 65 pounds, she determined that being mad at the Hutus and harboring revenge would do no good. She realized that the words of the Lord's Prayer were the words Jesus told her to pray, and she chose to obey her Lord. She grew to believe that as long as people are living, they have the opportunity to choose to be different. She readily admits that she asked God to help her obey His Word and give her the power to forgive. Today, Immaculée ministers to others as a voice of one whose life demonstrates purposeful forgiveness.

My husband, Tom, has been on several trips to Rwanda and the Congo with an organization headquartered in Middle Tennessee called African Leadership. In fact, he is there right now as I am writing this book. I received this text from him today: "Just met with a group of teenage boys who were recruited into the child army, unimaginable horrors." He told me later that Joseph Kony's army recruitment tactics involved going into a village and rounding up young boys. The soldiers took the boys in groups of three, then gave a gun to one of the boys and told him to shoot his brother. When he refused, the soldier took his gun away and killed the boy who wouldn't shoot his brother. He then gave it to the next boy and told him to shoot the other one. Whichever boy was the last one standing became the army's new recruit.

The leaders of African Leadership have collected countless stories like Immaculée's of men, women, and children who are choosing forgiveness against all odds. If these people—after suffering atrocities like that—can find within themselves the power to forgive, I can too, and so can you.

Forgiveness and Spiritual Warfare

Forgiveness is not optional for the follower of Christ. It's actually one of the commands we can only obey if we are exercising our spiritual authority. Remember the steps to releasing God's spiritual authority on your battlefield?

Step 1: Deny yourself, take up your cross, and follow Jesus.
Step 2: Obey God's Word.
Step 3: Embrace humility.

When people offend you, they actually do you a favor. They draw you to the plate (that's softball talk for when the batter steps up to bat), and they pitch you a curve ball so that you can take a swing at it and round the bases. When the offense comes your way, swing away! Hit it hard, then run as fast as you can through first base.

First base: Deny yourself, take up your cross, and follow Jesus. I learned by watching my girls play softball that you're supposed to run *through* not *to* first base. This is to keep you running fast in order to get there before the ball does. In using our run-the-bases illustration, your running through first base involves choosing to refuse to collect the offense like a treasure and pack it away in a box. Let it go!

Deny yourself that treasure/offense collection. Don't even think about it! Be so determined to put others first that you just run all out. When your mind tries to switch to instant (or distant) replay, change the channel. Think on something better, perhaps one of the whatevers: "Whatever is true, whatever is noble, whatever is right, whatever is pure, whatever is lovely, whatever is admirable—if anything is excellent or praiseworthy—think about such things" (Philippians 4:8).

Second base: Obey God's Word. Determine that you will not hold a grudge or harbor resentment, bitterness, or ill will toward your offender. This includes never bringing the matter up again, especially not to him/her at the most strategic time when it might do its greatest harm to them. This also includes never mentioning it to innocent bystanders who may eagerly heap wood on your smoldering wound.

No, you may not even talk about the situation in the form of a prayer request.

"Peter came to Him and said, 'Lord, how many times could my brother sin against me and I forgive him? As many as seven times?'" (Matthew 18:21 HCSB).

In other words, how many times are we supposed to let the same person get away with doing us wrong?

One commentator said the rabbis of that day challenged people to forgive an offender three times. Kind of like our ball game illustration: Three strikes and you're out! So Peter might have thought he was being generous by more than doubling the number of times he might be expected to forgive. So when Jesus responded to Peter's question with this, "'I tell you, not as many as seven,' Jesus said to him, 'but 70 times seven'" (Matthew 18:22 HCSB), Peter was no doubt baffled by His answer.

Jesus went on to illustrate His answer by telling the parable of a man who had a major debt problem. He owed the king 10,000 talents, or the equivalent to 165,000 years of work to pay off the debt (if every penny went to debt reduction). In the lesson I taught my seventh grade girls at church, I read that Jesus was using hyperbole to make His point.

A talent was the highest denomination of currency at that time, and 10,000 was the largest number in the Greek language. A worker typically earned one denarius a day, and it took 6,000 denarii to equal one talent. To earn one talent, then would take about 16.5 years. And with a debt of 10,000 talents, it would take this debtor 165,000 years to pay off his debt![4]

Jesus used this parable to show us how huge our debt is toward God. Our debt is so large that we cannot even begin to work toward its payoff. But like the king in the parable, God forgave us our debt when Jesus chose to pay it himself. Jesus not only died in our place, but He offered himself as the perfect sacrifice for our sin. We could die on a cross and it would deliver nothing. Our lives are blemished by sin, while Jesus' life was not. Jesus paid the debt we could never pay.

In Jesus' story, the king freed the man from his enormous debt. But rather than extend that same forgiveness to others, the man went to another man who owed him money. This second man's debt was microscopic compared to the first man's debt. He owed the freed man 100 denarii, which was about three months' wages. Three months vs. 165,000 years. How absurd is that?!

And yet, we do this every time we refuse to forgive others after all that God has done to forgive us. In order to exercise this powerful weapon of forgiveness, we must choose to obey God. And God commands us to forgive others.

Third base: Embrace humility. Once you've determined to deny yourself by refusing the temptation to make a treasure chest of offenses, and obey God by extending forgiveness to others, understand that you are never more like Jesus than when you choose to forgive. Who better knows what it's like to be offended, to have His rights violated, and to be taken complete advantage of?

I absolutely loved the illustration the writer used in this lesson on forgiveness (the one I taught to my seventh grade Sunday school class). He said to imagine you are holding three bills in your hand. Each bill represents a person who has hurt you and "owes" you because of the offense. The small bill, say $5, represents the one who hurt you in a minor way. They might not even be aware that something they said offended you. The $20 bill represents someone with whom you might have an ongoing struggle, that ornery person who serves as what my mother always called "heavenly sandpaper." The $100 bill represents the one who caused you enormous pain. The writer challenged the reader to "tear up the bill in your mind and let the person off the hook."[5]

I loved this illustration because it acknowledges that forgiveness does cost you something. But even though the cost of forgiveness might be high (it certainly was for God), it is well worth the investment.

Forgiveness Disarms the Enemy

Satan knows how to push your buttons. He's got a keen awareness of your soft spots. The devil understands human nature, and he knows that when your emotional energy and attention are consumed with a crisis, you are stretched thin. It's in those times that he pulls out the stops and unleashes his attack. I promise you he will give you plenty of opportunities to exercise your power to forgive. You will have the chance to forgive yourself, your family, your friends, your co-workers, your church members, even God. When you seize the opportunity to be like Christ and choose forgiveness, you dodge Satan's fiery darts. But when you choose not to forgive, you put aside this most powerful weapon and end up outflanked and undone.

You are not like Jesus when you choose to harbor an offense.

Jesus never did that.

You are not like Jesus when you refuse to forgive.

Jesus never did that.

You are not like Jesus when you nurse a grudge, cultivate a root of bitterness, or stockpile revenge.

Jesus never did any of that.

When you walk in unforgiveness, you go places Jesus never went. When you go places Jesus never went, you enter areas that are hostile to believers. When you enter areas that are hostile to believers, you get all confused. When you get all confused, you lose your bearings. When you lose your bearings, you lose your way. When you lose your way, wrong seems right and right seems wrong. When wrong seems right and right seems wrong, you do the wrong things thinking they are right. When you do the wrong things, thinking they are the right things, you mistake the conviction of the Holy Spirit for persecution. When you mistake conviction for persecution you are all kinds of messed up!

The enemy loves to offend you. It's one of his favorite baits! Don't be deceived.

Every offense delivers you the opportunity to crucify the flesh and release the resurrection power of the Holy Spirit. Forgiveness ushers God's power and His glory into the depths of your most difficult relationships with the most hard-hearted people. By extending forgiveness, you sometimes create cracks in the walls they've built around their hearts.

Forgiveness Step by Step

I don't know the specific battles you are fighting in your home, but I can almost guarantee you that no matter what they are, those conflicts have given you many opportunities to choose forgiveness. When you are given the opportunity to forgive, be ready with an action plan. Here's one I've discovered. It was created by a man who has dedicated his life's work to the ministry of forgiveness: Everett Worthington, a professor at Virginia Commonwealth University.

Just after Dr. Worthington completed his first book on forgiveness, his seventy-six-year-old mother was sexually violated and killed in her home in south Knoxville, Tennessee. Five years after that, Worthington's brother, who never recovered from his mother's brutal death, committed suicide. Dr. Worthington confessed that even though he was dedicated to teaching people the power of forgiveness, his mother's death ushered him in to a new depth of understanding just how difficult forgiveness can be. The rage he experienced the day her body was discovered, while understandable to us, was not acceptable to him.

Dr. Worthington eventually forgave his mother's killer (a teenage boy who beat her to death with a crowbar). But when his brother committed suicide, Worthington blamed himself. In the years following his brother's death, Dr. Worthington confessed that forgiving himself was much harder even than forgiving his mother's killer. That journey toward forgiveness led to his more recent book, *Moving Forward: Six Steps to Forgiving Yourself and Breaking Free From the Past.*

Dr. Worthington created the REACH method of forgiveness. You can learn more about the REACH method of forgiveness and even download a free leader's manual and participant's manual at www .people.vcu.edu/~eworth. The goal of this program is for people to "REACH an experience of lasting *emotional* forgiveness."[6]

Dr. Worthington defines two types of forgiveness:

1. Decisional forgiveness is defined as "deciding (even if you don't say it aloud) that you will not seek revenge against and not avoid but will try (as much as it is up to you) to put the relationship back on the pre-offense footing."
2. Emotional forgiveness is defined as "the degree to which you actually feel that your emotions have become less negative and more positive toward the person who offended or harmed you."[7]

Then, Dr. Worthington identifies five steps to forgiveness. I have taken the following information from *Becoming a More Forgiving Christian: Participant Manual* and rewritten it in my own words, sprinkling in my own thoughts along the way.

R=Recall the hurt. Remember what happened, what was said, how it was said, who was there, and how you felt. But don't camp out there.

E=Empathize with (and sympathize with, feel compassion for, and love) the one who hurt you. In order to do this, consider a time when you hurt someone. Recall your thoughts, your feelings, and your actions. Use this experience to entertain the thought that the one who hurt you might also have had thoughts and feelings that created what he/she considered good reasons for his/her behavior.

A personal note: When I was faced with the opportunity to forgive someone for his heinous behavior, I failed to consider this step. I didn't want to empathize with him, and to be quite honest, I didn't want to forgive him. I begged God to cease gravity's law for him and hurl him into space. When God didn't answer that prayer the way I wanted Him to, I shared my wound with anyone who'd listen and let their compassion fill my little pity pool where I found myself content to splash about a bit.

The longer I refused to forgive him, the greater his offense grew *in my thoughts.* The more I remembered his behavior, the more monstrous he became *in my mind.* It took me a long time to realize that I'd let the devil dance on my bitterness and take a very real man with a very real heart and mind, whose sin was forgiven by a very real Savior, and turn him into a beast. When I finally submitted this man to Christ, He invited me to see him as a boy. The mother heart in me broke for the little boy who was wounded by others, and who never had the privilege of processing his pain. Finally, I was able to empathize with him.

Dr. Worthington encourages us to consider whether or not we want our lives to revolve around our wound. Do you really want to be a victim the rest of your life? In order to become a forgiving person, you must determine to recognize God's providence (His working all things together for good) in your pain. Consider Joseph, Job, Stephen, and most of the apostles who were martyred for their faith. Why not look for how God might work redemption in your story?

A=Give an altruistic gift of forgiveness. I'll confess I had to look up the word *altruistic.* According to Dr. Worthington, "altruism is unselfish behavior to aid another person."[8] Dr. Worthington is telling us to give the gift of forgiveness because the perpetrator needs it, not because he's worthy, or deserving, or necessarily interested in receiving it.

Isn't this what Jesus did for us? Isn't this what Jesus did for all mankind? Think about it. Jesus died for all sinners. He died for the Auca Indians who killed Elisabeth Elliot's husband, the Hutu warriors who macheted countless people to death, and the teenage boy who killed a seventy-six-year-old woman with a crowbar. Jesus died for the adulterer, the child molester, the terrorists who piloted the commercial planes into the World Trade Center, and the person in your life who committed the unimaginable against you and stole what was precious from you.

Jesus gave an altruistic gift of forgiveness to every man and woman, boy and girl. If we are going to follow Him, we must do the same.

One of the ways Worthington guides you to give your altruistic gift of forgiveness is to remember a time when *you* were given an altruistic gift of forgiveness and recall your gratitude for such an undeserved gift. This gratitude for what you received (undeserved) will fuel your emotions to follow your decision to offer the same gift to another. This reminds me of a Bible verse I saw printed on the walls of the Rockefeller Center in Manhattan: "From everyone who has been given much, much will be required" (Luke 12:48 NASB).

C=Commit to the forgiveness you experienced. In this step, Worthington encourages us to share with others what we've done. "I have forgiven _____ for _____." Evaluate what percentage of your heart accompanies your decision to forgive. At this point it doesn't matter if it's 10 percent or 100 percent; the important thing is to know what you're feeling.

I want to take a minute right here to discuss a common misconception that God forgives and then forgets our transgressions. Hebrews 8:12 says, "I will forgive their wickedness and remember their sins no more." What this means is that God chooses to forgive so completely that He will never, ever give a moment's thought to the sins that He's forgiven. The blood of Jesus was enough to satisfy God's holiness, and when we ask His forgiveness, He never allows that sin to stand between us. To think that God actually forgets our sins might imply that God wanted to remember them and can't. By His very nature, there is nothing God cannot do, except break a promise. Therefore, God didn't know something about us, and then not know something about us. He still knows every sin we've ever committed, He just chooses to give those sins none of His attention. Their debt has been paid in full.

While we cannot forget the wrongs that have been done to us, we can choose to release them to God. We can let the sin go in such a way that we never allow the sin to stand between us and the person who wronged us. To commit to the forgiveness you experienced is to choose to offer another the same forgiveness that you have been offered. This is the fulfillment of Jesus' command in Matthew 6:14–15: "For if you forgive others for their transgressions, your heavenly Father will also forgive you. But if you do not forgive others, then your Father will not forgive your transgressions" (NASB).

Remember, your debt was the equivalent of 165,000 years of wages, and theirs might be no more than three months.

Don't mistake forgiving someone with allowing someone to continually mistreat or abuse you. To remain in an abusive relationship is to cling to distorted affections, to cower to fear of the unknown, and to continue in spiritual bondage. True forgiveness will establish healthy boundaries at the same time. If you are in an abusive relationship, please seek help from a trusted friend, pastor, or counselor. Get to a place where you and your children (if you have children) are safe, and work through the dynamics of your relationship from a safe distance.

H=Hold on to forgiveness when you doubt. I enjoyed reading Worthington's instructions on how to hold on to forgiveness. He says to ask God to show you what He loves about the person you forgave, and then reflect on what characteristic of God that might illuminate. He also urges the participants to identify ways that God has blessed them today.

Forgiveness as a Weapon of War

When you forgive, you completely disarm your enemy. You see people as they really are, and you exercise the power to be like Christ in the world today. When you forgive, you shine the light of the gospel not only on the recipient of your gift (who may not receive it) but also on everyone who knows you, and on those who know what you've endured. When you forgive, you take what the devil meant for harm and allow God to transform it into good.

Forgive until you can forgive with your eyes closed.

Forgive until you can forgive without your hands on the handlebars.

Forgive on one foot; forgive blindfolded and handcuffed.

Forgive in the morning; forgive in the afternoon; forgive as the sun goes down.

Forgive because it's the right thing to do, not because it's easy.

QUESTIONS TO CONSIDER

1. Who has given you the opportunity to exercise forgiveness?
2. What most compels you to forgive?
3. When and how have you been forgiven?

13

The Devil Doesn't Want You to Know the Power of the Holy Spirit

"When I was a little girl, I . . ." This is one of my four-year-old grand-daughter's favorite ways to begin a conversation. Most of the time Misty follows that statement with great detail over something she's heard us say about her early childhood (before four). Well, in Misty fashion, when I was a little girl, there was a fun little show on television called *Casper the Friendly Ghost*. It featured a sweet little ghost who was kind, cuddly, and always getting into some sort of mischief.

That friendly little ghost grew into my early concept of the Holy Spirit. Wasn't that clever of Satan to give me that visual? I was never taught much about the Holy Spirit. I just knew that He was good, He was for me, He was with me, and He was somehow a part of the triune God.

When I was in seminary, I tried to explain Him to a group of inner-city kids at a park in Fort Worth, Texas. I took an apple and peeled it, explaining that the peeling was like Jesus (God who became flesh and lived on earth with us), then I cut apart the meat of the apple and told them this was like the Holy Spirit (God who comes to live inside our hearts), and revealed to them the core (God the Father who is at the very center of all). I explained that although the apple is one fruit, these three distinct parts have different functions. It seemed to make sense at the time.

I'm still learning about the power of the Holy Spirit, and as I do, I realize that Satan doesn't want me to recognize His power or His presence in my life. The devil can't do a thing about the reality of the Holy Spirit, nor can he do a thing about God's gracious gift of the Holy Spirit. All he can do is keep you ignorant of the power of the Holy Spirit that rests quietly in your heart today.

So with an increasing awareness of my desperate dependence on His power in my life, I am going to unveil the truth about the Holy Spirit so that you can experience the power of His presence on your battlefield today.

The devil doesn't want you to know what I'm about to tell you, so take a minute to pause right now and pray. Close your eyes, listen to the sounds around you, consider all that is real that you hardly ever take time to acknowledge. (I'm writing on the porch today at my "laughing place" in the Blue Ridge Mountains. I just shut my eyes. I heard the bees—which are diving at me every once in a while—the wind, several different kinds of birds both singing and fluttering their wings, and crickets.) Ask God to give you ears to hear, eyes to see, a mind to understand, and a heart to receive the truth about the Holy Spirit. Tell Him you trust that He will keep His word to you. Now, read this promise aloud: "So if you sinful people know how to give good gifts to your children, how much more will your heavenly Father give the Holy Spirit to those who ask him" (Luke 11:13 NLT). Amen.

The Reality of the Spirit in You

Jesus told His disciples that it was good for Him to leave them; for once He was gone, He would send them the Holy Spirit (John 16:7). He explained to them that they would know the Holy Spirit because they had lived with Him, but that the day would come when the Holy Spirit would live *in* them (John 14:17).

Jesus said the Holy Spirit's presence on earth would be better than His bodily presence.

Jesus said the Holy Spirit's dwelling on earth would be *inside* the lives of His disciples.

Now, I don't know about you, but to be quite honest, there are many days when I would rather have Jesus in the flesh than the Holy Spirit in the . . . *spirit*. That's how I feel, but because I choose to believe God's Word is true, I have to agree with what it says. If Jesus said the Holy Spirit's presence in my life is even better than the bodily presence of Jesus by my side, the Holy Spirit's presence in my life *is* better. And since Jesus said the Holy Spirit lives in me, the Holy Spirit lives *in* me, no matter how I might feel or what I might think might contradict that reality. This thought process, by the way, is a technique in battle that you can continually develop. We can call it "choosing to believe what God says is true."

Most churchgoers don't have a clue about who the Spirit of God is and have not experienced what He does. This mystery is one the devil keeps most hidden from most believers most of the time. And as long as life delivers gumdrops and lollipops, you can remain ignorant of the Holy Spirit's presence and be inexperienced in the exercise of His power. It's only when life delivers heartache and disappointment that you begin to hunger for more of God and long for His presence and power in your life. So thank God right now for using spiritual warfare as an invitation for you to experience more of Him. Without the heartache or disappointment you might be facing today, you would not have this desire.

Don't skip this. Thank Him.

The Work of the Spirit in You

The Holy Spirit is not *What* but *Who*. The Holy Spirit is the personal presence and power of God in me. As I yield to Him,

He becomes the personal presence and power of God in the world around me. To the degree that I trust Him, and in direct proportion to the amount of His heart that I make my own, He becomes the personal presence and power of God in the world beyond me.

If Satan can keep you thinking of the Holy Spirit as a friendly little ghost, you will never experience His presence or His power. Choose this moment to dismiss Casper. Dismiss the vapor-like image you might have had of the Holy Spirit. Let the dove fly away. (The dove represents the Spirit of God because this was the physical form of the Spirit that God chose to use when Jesus was baptized. See John 1:32–34.) Release any other ghostlike or creature image you might have of the Holy Spirit.

Now replace that with the image of a man. Picture this man in a robe if that helps, in coveralls or blue jeans if that's better. See Him looking at you, smiling at you, stretching His arms wide to embrace you.

The image I have in my mind came from a stained-glass window in the church I attended as a child; it was the image of Jesus with His arms open wide beckoning me to come to Him. What do you imagine? Perhaps you see a warrior, battle-ready with eyes like fire, muscles tensed and sword raised high. You might see Jesus as a loving man sitting on a stone and listening intently to a small boy (which describes a tapestry I have hanging in the foyer of my home). Invite God to give you a picture of the Holy Spirit that will convince you that He is a person.

The person of the Spirit unites you with God and transforms you daily into the image of Christ. The moment you accepted Jesus' gift of salvation, the Holy Spirit came into your life. You became a brand-new person because of His penetration into your spiritual DNA. The effects of His presence might not have been as evident as you would like, but He is always there. He is patient and persistent. He is diligent and determined. He is constant and consistent. He convicts you of sin, reminds you of truth, removes you from the world, and comforts you in grief.

You can resist Him and you can grieve Him, but you cannot remove Him. He seals you for the day of Christ (2 Corinthians 1:21–22).

Jesus called the Holy Spirit "another advocate" (John 14:16). An advocate is one who defends, comforts, supports, and strengthens. The Holy Spirit does all of these things for you. He is ever-present (Psalm 46:1), which means He is never absent (Psalm 139:8). He is always for you (Romans 8:31), which means He is never against you (John 3:17). He comforts you (2 Corinthians 1:3–5), He strengthens you (Philippians 4:13), He provides for you (Philippians 4:19), and He completes the work He began in you (Philippians 1:6). I could go on and on and on and on.

The Holy Spirit is a person. He is a powerful person. He is able! He is willing! And He is alive *in* you.

The Power of the Spirit in You

When you allow the Holy Spirit to fill you with His presence, your life will give evidence of His power.

You will experience supernatural peace amid the chaos (Philippians 4:7).

You will demonstrate supernatural endurance and patience as you confidently walk through trials (Colossians 1:11).

You will be alert and clear-headed when everyone around you is confused (1 Thessalonians 5:5–7).

You will hold fast to truth, even encouraging others and giving them hope (2 Thessalonians 2:15–16).

You will love God through loving others, helping them, and continuing to help them (Hebrews 6:10).

Your quality of life, attitudes, and actions will show who you belong to and how you are at rest in His presence (1 John 3:18–19).

Sign me up!!! I want more of all of that, don't you? Here's how to experience all of these things and more.

Be filled with the Spirit of God.

You are full of the Spirit when you let Him be fully in control. If I were to sit across the table from you this minute and ask you this question, what would your answer be?

Who is in charge of your life?

Are you? Are they (your children, spouse, friends, employers, appetites, and material possessions)? Or is He?

The Nemesis of the Spirit Is the Flesh

The devil will downplay the power of the Holy Spirit in you. But all he has to deal with is your flesh and your imagination. If he can distract you from God through preoccupation with the flesh, he can keep you from connecting with the power of the Holy Spirit. And the thing about fleshly appetites is that they are rooted in spiritual yearnings. I may yearn for comfort (something the Holy Spirit delivers) and find some measure of comfort in chocolate. The ingredients in chocolate trigger the comfort chemicals in my body, and for a moment or two, I receive what I'm seeking in the temporary fix. But only the Spirit can deliver comfort that truly satisfies.

The same could be true in my search for courage, or insight, or stress release, or . . . you name whatever it is you're looking for. God intends that we enjoy the nourishment He provides, but He longs for us to come to Him for our deepest needs and most desperate longings. The Holy Spirit will release His power in us when we look to Him and not the substitutes Satan and the world offer.

The best attack against the flesh is to fast. Spend a designated period of time denying your flesh some pleasure. Fast from solid food or from food altogether. Fast from television, or social media, or caffeine, or chocolate. Fast when you realize the appetites of your flesh have been fed so much they've grown out of control. A good fast will subdue the flesh and make it bow down to the Spirit. Fasting does so much more, and is the secret to many spiritual breakthroughs. I encourage you to study the spiritual discipline of fasting and practice it on a regular basis.

The Life of the Spirit in You

Only an empty vessel can be filled. The bad news is that God will not fill what is not empty. The good news is that there are only two parts of you that have to be emptied: your head and your heart.

Give God your head. Choose to agree with Him regarding what is and is not true. The only way you will be able to do this is to read His Word. Know what the Bible has to say about marriage, parenting, sin, faith, immorality, and endurance. Read God's Word and let His Word be your authority on life.

Be willing to admit that your way of thinking is faulty. Acknowledge that even what you think is right could be wrong. "Lean not on your own understanding" (Proverbs 3:5). When you discover that you were mistaken, have the courage to admit you were wrong, and to change your way of thinking.

Remind yourself daily that you don't know all there is to know about a situation—or anything, for that matter. You cannot pass judgment on others because you don't truly know their hearts. You can't project the outcome of a problem because you have no way of knowing what the future holds. You can't even process the events of the past because you don't have all the pieces of the puzzle. Remind yourself daily that you are not as smart as you sometimes fool yourself into thinking you are.

Analyze your thoughts regarding the battle you are fighting right now. Which of these thoughts agrees with God's Word? Which of them were birthed out of your own understanding? Which ones have resulted from judgments and assumptions? Which have popped up because of circumstances? Here are some thoughts I've had lately:

- She's falling further and further away from God.
- He's never going to change.
- She's stuck, and I don't know a thing that will help her.

For the sake of practice, let's analyze my thoughts:

- She's falling further and further away from God. How can I know that? Perhaps what looks like her running from God is actually Him steering her smack-dab into His arms!
- He's never going to change. What Scripture supports that thought? Here's one that defeats it: "Anyone who is among the living has hope" (Ecclesiastes 9:4).
- She's stuck, and I don't know a thing that will help her. So what? She's never going to get better if I'm her only hope! But God, on the other hand, can do the unthinkable, the never-done-before, the impossible!

See how this works? Once you analyze your thoughts, agree with God that He has given you the mind of Christ (1 Corinthians 2:14–16). Thank God for the filling of the Spirit, who teaches you all things (John 14:26), who will guide you into all the truth (16:13), and who gives you supernatural discernment (1 John 4:1–6). Learn to count on Him to tell you great and unsearchable things you do not know (Jeremiah 33:3).

Choose to believe what God says is true.

Give God your heart. For some of us, it's the heart that's harder to let go. But if you want to walk in alignment, you will keep your head and your heart together. Hearts without heads are reckless, and heads without hearts are sometimes cold.

I discussed the head first, because your head can lead your heart far better than your heart can lead your head. Your heart is a good follower, but a terrible leader. Nevertheless, it's the heart that ultimately controls you, so it is absolutely necessary to give God your heart if you want to be filled with His Spirit.

Andrew Murray said this:

> As a man's heart is, so is he before God. . . . Very many Christians have no sense of the great difference between the Christianity of the mind and the Christianity of the heart, and the former is far more diligently cultivated than the latter. They do not know how infinitely greater the heart is than the mind. . . . It is with the heart that man believes

and comes in touch with God. It is in the heart that God has given His Spirit to be the presence and the power of God working in us. In all our faith, it is the heart that must trust, love, worship and obey.[1]

I've heard this truth stated like this: "I finally made the connection between my heart and my head." Oh, for this eighteen-inch journey to be completed in the lives of multitudes who profess to follow Christ! I've known Jesus with my head for as long as I can remember, but when I received Him with my heart, my life radically changed.

To give God your heart is to choose to allow Him to rearrange your desires, passions, appetites, and affections. When you allow Him full access to your heart, God stretches your perspective beyond life on earth (just as He did with Peter when he was reprimanded for declaring that Jesus should not die). He reorients your life to center around Him rather than yourself (or your children or your spouse). We're about to discuss this more in the next few chapters of this book. He even uses pain and suffering to discipline you and develop strength in your heart (see Romans 5:3–4; Hebrews 12:10–11).

Giving God your heart is quite easy when you and God agree, but extremely difficult when you don't. Be encouraged by this: The Holy Spirit works this yielding of your heart in you. He's mindful of your weakness and more than able to overcome it.

The devil doesn't want you to know about the Holy Spirit because he knows the power of God better than you do. The devil knows that when you yield yourself to Him, he will be soundly defeated.

"'Not by might nor by power, but by my Spirit,' says the Lord Almighty" (Zechariah 4:6).

QUESTIONS TO CONSIDER

1. Does your life give evidence of the power of God?
2. What thoughts do you need to give to God?
3. What attitudes, desires, ambitions, or affections do you need to give to God?

PART 4

Desperate Times Call for Desperate Measures

Sin is what you do when your heart is not satisfied with God.

—John Piper, *Future Grace*

14

Tear Down the High Places

Earlier this year I accepted the challenge to read through the entire Bible in ninety days. This flyover of the Bible gave me some new insights into God's Word. Because I read it from start to finish so quickly, I became aware of overarching themes and patterns in the collection of sixty-six books that comprise the canonized Scripture.

As I was speeding through the Old Testament period of the divided kingdom (1 and 2 Kings; 1 and 2 Chronicles) I was struck by the succession of king after king who either obeyed or disobeyed God. Their obedience led to blessing and their disobedience led to the absence of God's blessing on their kingdom. Each king's life was summarized with a statement that went something like this: "*King so-and-so* obeyed God and did what was pleasing in His sight like his father David did before him, and God *did something great* for the kingdom." Or, "*King so-and-so* disobeyed God and did what was evil in His sight unlike his father David did before him, and God *allowed something terrible* to happen to the kingdom."

Then in the middle of all these kings, I came upon Amaziah and this serious indictment against him:

"[Amaziah] did what was right in the eyes of the Lord, *but not wholeheartedly.*"

2 Chronicles 25:2 (emphasis mine)

I discovered that Amaziah's devotion to God was blemished by his refusal to tear down the "high places." With that discovery came a solemn conviction that, at the end of my life on earth, the same might be said about me: "Leighann did what was pleasing in the Lord's sight, but not wholeheartedly."

What about you?

It's this less-than-absolute devotion to God that keeps giving the Enemy an edge in the battles he wages against us.

What Are the High Places?

In Amaziah's day, the high places were altars built on hills and mountains where pagan gods were worshiped. They often consisted of altars for burnt sacrifices, shrines, and sacred objects, such as stone pillars or carved wooden poles. The high places were used for idol worship, and God was—and is today—strongly opposed to idolatry.

At first glance, I didn't think I was guilty of idolatry. When I traveled to India, China, and Japan, I saw what idol worship looks like. In those lands there are temples to false gods. In India, the gods might even appear in fields, and in China there were idols on street corners. But in my study I found this definition of idol worship: "Your god is anything or anyone who occupies your thoughts and time more than the true God."[1]

Idolatry can be anything that prevents you from being completely committed to God. When I discovered this definition of idolatry, my heart sank.

I am guilty of idol worship.

For there have been people and even ideas, dreams, and goals that I've allowed to occupy my thoughts and time more than God. So I began to consider the "high places" that we worship in our world today. We worship the "isms": materialism, humanism, intellectualism, emotionalism, legalism. And they include the "itys" as well: religiosity, sensuality, and celebrity.

Can you think of more?

Some of us make high places out of health and fitness, the pursuit of eternal youth, sensual indulgences (drinking, eating, recreating, or working), worldly success, wealth, and power. Our relationships, and even ministry, can become "high places." What about comfort—lives of ease, void of suffering? The desire for peace can become a high place.

I wrestled, especially with this phrase mentioned over and over again: "The high places were not removed." I realized that I could be a good girl of God and still fall short of experiencing *all* the blessings that God has for me if I didn't deal with the high places in my life.

Satan knows that when we erect high places, we hinder God's blessing in and through our lives.

Do you want to be like so many of those biblical kings who experienced a measure of peace and prosperity but only in proportion to their limited obedience? Or do you want to be like Hezekiah, who did the hard and courageous work of removing the high places and therefore experienced the power and love of God in full measure? (Read Hezekiah's story in 2 Chronicles 30–32.) I want to be like Hezekiah.

I would be doing you a disservice if I didn't remind you that Hezekiah faced a season of life when, even after he pleased God with his obedience, his enemies challenged him. But rather than it being a disastrous time in Hezekiah's life, it became an opportunity for God's glory to shine. You will find this story in 2 Chronicles 32. Sometimes God's blessings come in unusual packages.

God Is Not a Genie

A sure sign of idolatry in our lives is the subject of our prayers. Some of us are so driven by our need for comfort, peace, and joy that we press God down into a bottle and keep Him there until we decide we need His help. Once our circumstances get beyond our control, we bring Him out. It reminds me of the old television sitcom *I Dream of Jeannie.* Cute little Jeannie popped in and out of her little bottle and created all kinds of mischief for her astronaut "master." She had magical power, but he had authority over her.

We sometimes pray as if we rule God like Tony ruled Jeannie. God isn't a genie! The God we serve is the Lord of the universe, the Maker of heaven and earth, the Supreme Being, the Ultimate Authority, the Giver and Sustainer of life! He will never be pressed into the bottle of our limited understanding, our earthly passions, our faulty thinking, or our deceived perceptions or affections. God will be *God,* and if we want to experience His power in our lives, we will rid ourselves of idol worship. We will tear down the high places.

In his article "Idolatry Is Alive Today," Ed Stetzer wrote,

> Idolatry is not just a pagan issue. It is not just an Old Testament or Jewish issue. It is a human issue. Is it that a 12-inch tall piece of wood or bronze can do something bad to us? Or is it that we do something awful to ourselves when we place adoration and attention that should go to God in other things? When it comes to idolatry, the danger is not in an item . . . it is in us. It was John Calvin who said our heart is an idol factory. In a fallen world, people constantly seek things they can worship, even though the Creator is before us in plain view. We are all looking for something to worship and serve. Idols come easy, but go hard. There is a consistent theme about idolatry throughout the Scriptures—and in our lives as well.[2]

Stetzer went on to say that idols have to be torn down and destroyed. We have to take an aggressive approach to removing the idols in our lives.

The question is not "Do I have any idols in my life?" but rather "What are the idols in my life?" Once you identify the idols in your life, examine the high places you've built and determine to remove them.

What Are the High Places in Your Life?

The devil doesn't want you to identify the idols in your life. He wants you to ignore the high places and pretend they are okay. He'll convince you that since you pray, read your Bible, and give financially to the church, you're a good Christian. But God is a jealous God, and He created you to be most satisfied when you live in constant awareness that He, and only He, delivers what your heart desires.

Don't miss that profound truth: **God wants you to live in constant awareness that He, and only He, delivers what your heart desires.**

Most of your spiritual battles are fought over misperceptions of God. The devil hints at God's motives, then appeals to your flesh, and eventually convinces you that God is not who He says He is, and that He cannot or will not deliver what your heart longs for. He causes you to doubt God and step away from your proper position of absolute surrender to Him and complete dependence on Him.

An idol is anything or anyone you love more than God.

An idol can be something God *has to do for you* in order for you to be pleased with Him.

When you think of an idol as something or someone you love more than God, it ceases to exist in the form of a golden image. Suddenly it becomes *the thing*.

John Piper calls the idol in our lives "the thing."

> What is an idol? Well, it is the thing. It is the thing loved or the person loved more than God, wanted more than God, desired more than God, treasured more than God, enjoyed more than God. It could be a girlfriend [boyfriend/wife/husband, or lover]. It could be good grades. It could be the approval of other people. It could be success in business. It could be sexual stimulation. It could be

a hobby or a musical group that you are following or a sport or your immaculate yard. . . . Your own looks could be an idol. It could be anything.[3]

An idol could be your own children.

What Happens When We Make Idols of Our Children?

I'd been praying for over seven years; one Scripture verse—a promise God gave me at the outset of my journey—numerous tears, countless hours, and hundreds of pages in several journals. The battle was fierce, and with every setback my resolve increased. I grew to be consumed with my longing, and I took my stand in the gap and set my eyes on the Lord.

Or so I thought.

As the Holy Spirit continued to woo me into a deeper understanding of idolatry, I had to confess that I'd let her, my precious flesh-and-blood proof that God answers prayer, my firstborn child, my daughter, become my idol. *She* was my high place.

I wasn't satisfied with God *alone*. I was satisfied with God *if only* . . .

"Lord, if only you would rescue her, establish her, redeem her, restore her . . ."

The list went on and on and on.

I was appalled when I realized that I'd turned my heartache into an idol. I'd taken the daughter God had given me and exalted her higher than Him in my heart and my mind. God was too slow in answering my prayers; He was absent, and her demise was not. She'd be ashamed if she knew I considered her so frail that I took on her burden, that I elevated her above her siblings and her dad (my husband), and ministry. She'd be the first to tell me to stop, not to worry, that she could take care of herself! And yet I treated her (in my mind and heart) as if she were a newborn baby and her very existence depended on my all-consuming attention to the details of her life.

God was kind but persistent in dealing with me. He got my attention with Amaziah's sad epitaph. Then He led me on this study of the high places and idol worship. Once I realized my own daughter was my idol, God led me to another article, where I read this:

> If we put our children on the throne of our hearts, the clock is ticking before everything blows up. That is because idols are always a cover-up for *self-worship*. When children become our idols, it means they become the means to our meaning. The sad thing about the dad who won't get off his son's back at football practice is that the dad's significance is so bound up in the success of his son that he can't imagine failure. Under the guise of loving his son, he actually creates unbearable pressure and is using his son for his own advantage. Everyone loses.[4]
>
> Jonathan Parnell

I have to confess that I worshiped the idol of my child and just about killed her (and me) with that worship. Is your idol your child? Has his behavior caused you to be consumed by his situation? Do you eat, breathe, and sleep thinking about him and his trouble? If you do, you have made an idol out of your child.

And God wants you to know that He hates idolatry.

What Happens When We Fail to Worship God?

Idolatry leads to futility in your thinking and abandonment by God. Read Romans 1:21–32 to see the natural progression of idol worship.

Worship of something or someone other than God leads to . . .
Failure to recognize God's gifts, which leads to . . .
Thanklessness, which leads to . . .
Darkened and confused minds, which lead to . . .
Believing one is wise when really he is mistaken, which leads to . . .
Abandonment by God, which leads to . . .

Being consumed by vile and abominable desires, which lead to . . .

Sin.

And what is worse, those who worship idols eventually become so consumed by the objects of their affection that they forsake God altogether and encourage others to do the same. We are turned over to the futility of our minds. And God abandons us; then our foolish minds lead us astray and we suffer serious consequences as we live out our days on earth only to face God in heaven and realize what a waste we made of the opportunity we had to make a difference while we were here.

Are You Ready to Tear Down Some High Places?

Here's how all this came together for me. As I considered the high places, I realized that I'd made a high place out of my daughter. Once I realized that I'd allowed her to become an idol, I confessed my sin of idolatry.

"Lord, this is my *thing*! My high place . . . my idol! I don't want to be like Amaziah. I don't want to live my entire life doing what is pleasing in your sight but not wholeheartedly! Please forgive me for making a high place out of the precious gift you gave me!"

After I prayed and asked God to forgive me for allowing my child to consume me, I changed the way I prayed for her. I replaced prayers for deliverance with prayers of repentance.

"Father, forgive me for being so blind! I so built a high place out of a serious burden! This idol worship is detestable to you!"

I asked God to forgive her. I recognized how her sin stood as an offense to the holiness of God. Where before I begged Him to overlook her sins and not hold them against her, I realized that only by her acceptance of His grace would she be forgiven.

I became much more concerned about my offending a holy God than I was about God doing what I asked or not doing what I asked, and thereby offending me.

And the most remarkable thing began to happen. I began to understand that my circumstances were no longer anything to fret over in light of God's power and love. I began to disarm the Enemy. I'd inadvertently given Satan an edge on the battlefield by constructing, then failing to tear down, the high places.

Satan used my high places to hurl accusations my way: "Why would a loving God allow this to happen to you?"

Once I removed the high place, my darkened mind was illuminated with understanding. When the accuser accuses me now, I am ready with an explanation. I see very clearly what God is up to and where I fit into all of that.

Before, I was reasoning and angling and supposing and projecting. "If I do this, then . . ." or, "If only this, then . . ." Now I take all that energy I used to put into what Leighann can do and I channel it into my prayers. I put concerted effort into the activity of *being still*. As I still and quiet my soul, I let my heart soar beyond logic and reason into a new reality of "what only God can do." I pray and trust and hope and believe and anchor myself to the promises God has given me.

And then I recognize that the most powerful posture I can take is one of dominion over this matter on earth. For now there is no question as to what I want. I want God to be lifted up and His will to be done! Therefore, I have returned to God's original intent for my life: for me to find my complete satisfaction in Him alone. I have embraced fully my position *in Christ* and I declare that Satan is bound and His power is lost in this struggle over me.

Once I recognized that God will *never* step aside from His rightful place of glory and honor—I came to two conclusions:

1. Apart from God I can do absolutely *nothing*!
2. But with Him there is absolutely *nothing* I cannot do!

So I pray, I trust, I listen, and I obey whatever God wants me to do so that He receives the glory. It is just a matter of time until the Enemy realizes we've won this battle. And mark my words, soon we will collect the spoils of this victory.

Do you want to disarm the Enemy and take away his ability to deceive you?

Tear down your high places.

QUESTIONS TO CONSIDER

Here were some of the questions that I considered when I responded to the conviction that I had allowed high places to remain in me. Considering your answers to these questions will help you identify idolatry in your life.

1. Do we really detest our idols or do we accept them? Try to justify them? Or even exalt them? Is it possible that even a gift from God can become an idol? (I thought often of Abraham and Isaac when I pondered this question.)

2. Do we pray for forgiveness, recognizing that our idolatry is offensive to God? Or do we pray and beg God, "Just don't look!" (My granddaughter Misty says this to me when she is doing something wrong. She says, "Don't look at me, Nana!" And she gets mad if I refuse to look away.) Don't we do this when we bring our burdens before God and ask desperately for relief without first dealing with the enormous issue of this idol?

3. Do we intercede, "Father, forgive them" for our family members? Do we recognize that their sin is offensive to a holy God? Or do we beg God to bend His purposes, His person, and His promises to satisfy our need to lift our loved ones higher so that they escape the pain of their own poor choices?

15

Train Your Brain to Embrace the Mind of Christ

When God gave us the ability to reason and think for ourselves, He took a great risk. Knowing that we would often make the wrong choices, God nevertheless chose to let us have ownership of our own minds. When we choose to receive His gift of salvation and be intimately connected to Him, we freely give Him authority over us. As we walk in this new way of life, we learn to train our brains to yield and submit to His mind when it differs from ours. When we submit our thoughts to God, He gives us mighty weapons that knock down strongholds. The reasoning of God is not only different than human reasoning, but His reasoning is also better: "'For my thoughts are not your thoughts, neither are your ways my ways,' declares the Lord" (Isaiah 55:8).

In this chapter I am going to show you how to line your mind up with the mind of Christ so that you can access power to knock down, destroy, and demolish every obstacle that sets itself up against Christ. By the end of this chapter, you will know how to capture your thoughts and make them obedient to Christ.

Second Corinthians 10:3–5 serves as the basis of what I am teaching you:

> For though we live in the world, we do not wage war as the world does. The weapons we fight with are not the weapons of the world. On the contrary, they have divine power to demolish strongholds. We demolish arguments and every pretension that sets itself up against the knowledge of God, and we take captive every thought to make it obedient to Christ.

There are five steps to take to train your brain to have the mind of Christ, and three specific weapons God has given you to use when taking down strongholds. I'm going to share the five steps in this chapter and the three weapons in the following chapters. But before I share those five steps with you, I want to answer this question: What does it mean to have the mind of Christ?

What Does It Mean to Have the Mind of Christ?

To have the mind of Christ is to share the plan, the purpose, and the perspective of God in all things pertaining to life. It is to understand and join God's purpose in the world today, which is to bring glory to himself (remember our discussion of the glory of God in chapter 3). God accomplishes His purpose, thus bringing glory to himself, when He saves sinners and sanctifies saints. You are participating in the mind of Christ by reading this book. When you seek to know God, you are gaining the mind of Christ.

In most of our relationships, we are so focused on knowing our own minds that we don't develop the ability to get to know the other person's. We are also so busy giving them a piece of our minds that we don't make room to receive the pieces they are giving back to us. But in any relationship that is genuinely rewarding, you will share your mind with each other. You will not only expect your friend to know your mind, but you will be eager to know his as well.

Through the study of God's Word, through building relationships with other believers, through prayer, and even through reading books like this one, you are developing the mind of Christ. Scripture speaks of the mind of Christ in 1 Corinthians 2:

1. The mind of Christ is made known to you by the Spirit of God (the Holy Spirit) (2:10–12).
2. Spiritual truths are reserved for spiritual people. In other words, you must have received the Spirit of God in order to know the truths of God (2:13–15).
3. You are able to understand spiritual truths because you already have the mind of Christ (2:15–16).

Remember our discussion of the Holy Spirit in chapter 13? The Holy Spirit is not *What* but *Who*. He is a person who lives in you. All of who He is comes in to dwell within your mind, your heart, and your soul, eager to be expressed. The power of the Holy Spirit lives in you, and the presence of the Holy Spirit lives in you; therefore, the mind of the Spirit lives in you.

You already possess the mind of Christ.

His thoughts, plans, purposes, and passions are not somewhere "out there"; they are living in you. You come to understand them when you remove the obstacles that remain from your old way of life and become one with Him. Paul wrote to the church at Corinth, "Who has known the mind of the Lord so as to instruct him? But we have the mind of Christ" (1 Corinthians 2:16).

Before Christ came and died for our sins, then resurrected from the grave and secured our salvation, we could not possibly know the mind of God. But what was not possible before Christ is now possible through Christ. Today we can know the mind of Christ.

Train Your Brain to Embrace the Mind of Christ

The mind of Christ is in you! Take just a minute to let that true statement take root in your mind. There are five easy steps you must take to embrace the mind of Christ. (Okay, I may need to confess that these steps might not be easy but they are simple.) And when you embrace the mind of Christ you will win the battles for your home as effectively as if the Spirit of God were fighting them instead of you.

Don't forget that Zechariah said, "'Not by might nor by power, but by my Spirit,' says the Lord Almighty" (Zechariah 4:6).

Step 1: Choose to Live a Life of Resistance

Our natural tendency is to strive for lives of comfort and ease. We want to go along, get along, and live at peace with one another. Getting along with one another is a good thing, but if you compromise your convictions in order to keep peace, you have placed your happiness and earthly pleasure before God.

Peter was rebuked by Christ for putting his earthly affections ahead of God's eternal plans. You can read the story in Matthew 16. I wrote a chapter on this in *A Woman's Guide to Hearing God's Voice*, but I reference it as an example of what happens to us when our minds fall short of the glory of God. Perhaps Satan was allowed to sift Peter so that Peter would embrace the mind of Christ.

If you want to be ruled by the mind of Christ, overcome this predisposition to examine life from an earthly perspective. Where the world calls your pursuit of happiness an inalienable right, God calls you to a life of intentional strife.

This is not a life of unnecessary fighting and dissension, where you go out like the crusaders of old to kill the infidels. But it is a life of focus that solemnly acknowledges that conflict with the world, with unbelievers, with ideologies, and with philosophies will be inevitable.

Choose to live a life of resistance.

Step 2: Search for God in the Dark Places

I wrote an entire book on this step. *A Woman's Guide to Hearing God's Voice* is all about discovering God in the dark. There is a verse in Exodus that says this: "Moses approached the thick darkness where God was" (Exodus 20:21). A determination to live a life of resistance will lead you to and through many dark places. The conflict you may be going through right now (perhaps the one that compelled you to pick up this book) may be the very place you will discover the mind of Christ like you never knew it before.

Because you have chosen to live a life of resistance, search for God in the dark places.

Don't exhaust your mental and emotional strength searching for the light of comfort when God is wooing you into the dark. God is always on His throne, and no matter what you are going through, He is able to meet you where you are, draw you to himself, and execute the victory He has over Satan.

In *A Woman's Guide to Hearing God's Voice*, I shared a prayer a friend prayed over my husband and me when we were ushered into the dark place that has been my stomping grounds for several years.

> *O gracious Father, we know that you love our pastor and his wife. We know that nothing can come against them that hasn't first been brought before your throne. And although this situation they are in today is breaking their hearts, we believe that you have allowed it because you want to take them with you into the deep, dark, and secret places where your most valuable treasures are hidden. As you lead them in the dark, Lord, make them aware of your presence. And don't let their own suffering stop them from collecting every single treasure you have for them there.*[1]

Learn to love spiritual spelunking.

Step 3: Confess Your Sins

The power of confession is that it requires that you take notice of the discrepancies between your attitudes and actions and your beliefs and convictions. Confession exposes the attitudes and actions that are contrary to the mind of Christ. This is where you disarm the Enemy, whose intent is to sneak up on you and dull your sensitivity to the mind of Christ by gunking up your thinking process with unconfessed sin.

The unbeliever cannot understand spiritual truth because his mind is set on the things of this world. His thought patterns, his biases, his preconceived notions, are rooted in life apart from God. However, even though you are saved, you will also experience foggy thinking when the ways of this world seep into your mind and attempt to cloud the truth.

The other morning I picked up my granddaughters at their mother's place of work and started traveling toward home. That morning we had an unusually dense fog; I could barely see 100 feet around me. When Misty (four) looked out the windows of the car she said, "Nana, it's soggy this morning!" I had to agree, it was so soggy we couldn't see the stores, the schools, the church, and all of the other things we were accustomed to seeing on our way to my house. I explained to her that the clouds were hanging low and we were driving right through the middle of them.

Sin and disobedience cause the clouds of confusion to hang low in our lives. If we don't take the time to confess our sins, we end up straining to see God in the soggy, dense fog.

As preparation for people to receive Jesus' ministry, John the Baptist urged them to repent of their sins! By repenting of sin, their eyes would be opened and they would be able to see and know Jesus when they met Him. In order to know the mind of Christ, you must change the mind of you (the you apart from Christ). You must yield to the conviction of God in your heart and allow His truth to replace your lies. When what you believe disagrees with what God says in His Word, choose to go with God. In this way you embrace the mind of Christ.

The Bible speaks of the importance of confession:

> If we confess our sins, he is faithful and just and will forgive us our sins and purify us from all unrighteousness.
>
> 1 John 1:9

Repent, then, and turn to God, so that your sins may be wiped out, that times of refreshing may come from the Lord.

Acts 3:19

Then I acknowledged my sin to you and did not cover up my iniquity. I said, "I will confess my transgressions to the Lord." And you forgave the guilt of my sin.

Psalm 32:5

Here is a simple way to develop the habit of confession:

1. Sit down with pen and paper.
2. Pray and ask God to show you your sins.
3. Write each one on the paper.
4. As God reveals your sins to you, ask Him to forgive you.
5. Claiming the truth of God's Word, jot 1 John 1:9 over each sin.
6. Thank God for His forgiveness and His cleansing power.
7. Tear the list to shreds, burn it, or toss it in the trash. For when God forgives your sins, He chooses never to hold them against you again. (See Hebrews 8:12.)

Confess your sins daily. Sins are like trash; if you never empty the trash, the house is going to get smelly. Confession clears the clutter in your mind and in your heart. When you confess your sins, your practical theology matches your intellectual theology, and you dissolve any discrepancy. When the soggy, dense fog is burned away by the power of God's forgiveness, you will have greater insight into the mind of Christ.

Step 4: Focus on the Facts

The devil has one strategy, and that is deception. He will work constantly to woo you over to his way of thinking by challenging your faith. He will cast doubt on God's motives and His ways.

This is where God's Word comes into play! Jesus taught this step when he was praying for his disciples in John 17:

> My prayer is not for the world, but for those you have given me, because they belong to you. All who are mine belong to you, and you have given them to me, so they bring me glory. Now I am departing from the world; they are staying in this world, but I am coming to you. Holy Father, you have given me your name, now protect them by the power of your name so that they will be united just as we are. During my time here, I protected them by the power of the name you gave me. I guarded them so that not one was lost, except the one headed for destruction, as the Scriptures foretold.
>
> Now I am coming to you. I told them many things while I was with them in this world so they would be filled with my joy. I have given them your word. And the world hates them because they do not belong to the world, just as I do not belong to the world. I'm not asking you to take them out of the world, but to keep them safe from the evil one. They do not belong to this world any more than I do. Make them holy by your truth; teach them your word, which is truth. Just as you send me into the world, I am sending them into the world. And I give myself as a holy sacrifice for them so they can be made holy by your truth.
>
> vv. 9–19 NLT

Truth is the antidote to deception. God's Word is truth. When you read and study God's Word, when you memorize it and apply it to your life, you know the mind of Christ. Scripture tells us God's Word is

- Living and active—"For the word of God is living and active. Sharper than any double-edged sword, it penetrates even to dividing soul and spirit, joints and marrow; it judges the thoughts and attitudes of the heart" (Hebrews 4:12).
- Able to shed light—"Your word is a lamp for my feet, a light on my path" (Psalm 119:105).

• Able to stand the test of time—"No, I will not break my covenant; I will not take back a single word I said" (Psalm 89:34 NLT).

When you are on the battlefield, the circumstances surrounding you will seem to contradict God's Word. Anytime there seems to be a contradiction, invite God to place holy blinders over your eyes, and lead you through the waves of doubt. Jesus said "I tell you the truth" seventy-eight times in the Gospels. I've listed those references in the article titled "Scriptural References to Jesus Saying 'I Tell You the Truth'" at www.LeighannMcCoy .com/SpiritualWarfareTools.

There is a saying about the animal kingdom: "Eyes on the front, born to hunt; eyes on the side, born to hide." This is a reference to the distinction of prey or predator. Lions, for instance, have eyes on the front of their heads and are born hunters. Zebras have eyes on the sides of their heads and are prey.

Translate this into spiritual realities. When you have your eyes focused on Jesus, the author and perfecter of your faith (Hebrews 12:2 NASB), you are moving toward your win! "Eyes on front, born to hunt."

But if you shift your focus to the circumstances surrounding you, you will easily move from hunter to prey. Instead of remaining focused on the win you will be on the lookout for the next enemy attack. Your energy will be spent interpreting situations and predicting reasonable confidence in the projected outcomes. Granted, you are better able to protect yourself from harm, but you're also easily distracted and spooked.

Racehorses have eyes on the sides, but because they are bred to run and win, they wear blinders. These blinders serve to block out the distractions so that they will stay focused on what is in front of them. Jockeys know that their horses will run better if they can keep them from seeing the horses, crowds, and other commotion surrounding them.

In the same way, take up the spiritual blinders God has given you in His Word. Put His promises over your eyes and trust Him to prove himself faithful to them.

Too many Christian soldiers who ought to be warriors don't even hope to win the war. They just want to survive the skirmish. God called you to be a warrior, not a wimp. You are a predator, not prey.

"Eyes on the front, born to hunt!"

Step 5: Bear Your Cross

I learned a new thing today about cross-bearing. I've already written of the spiritual authority we exercise when we respond to Jesus' recruitment speech in Luke 9:23, "If anyone would come after me, let him deny himself and take up his cross daily and follow me" (ESV).

But there is a bit more to this invitation from our Savior and Lord.

You've heard people say, "Everyone has a cross to bear." When I hear that statement, I think of the burdens I bear, the trials I endure, and the heartaches I manage. The cross is a terrible thing; it's a place of suffering and death. I've mentioned already that the cross was perhaps Rome's cruelest form of execution (I don't know about that when I consider that Emperor Nero also served early Christians to wild animals, impaled them on poles, and lit them up at night to illuminate the road out of Rome to his vacation resort).

But in the heavenlies, the cross was much more than a place of suffering and shame. The cross was the place God's love ran deep. Jesus went to the cross willingly in absolute and resolute obedience to God. The wrath of God was satisfied on the cross because Jesus substituted himself as a vessel for sin. God poured the wrath of His holiness out on the sin of mankind without touching one hair on our heads. We deserved God's wrath; Jesus took our place. The cross was where the wrath of God's holiness met the love of God's holiness and the Lion of Judah lay down with the Lamb of Christ. God is both the Lion and the Lamb!

When we follow Jesus, we too must bear the cross. The cross is the place where our obedience to God is tested and made pure. The cross exposes the high places and idols we've allowed in our lives. The cross is where anything that is not holy is purged from our lives. The cross is the place we pray, "Not my will, but Thine be done." The cross is where we crucify the flesh and give ourselves fully to God. The pain of the cross for us is in dying to self.

But don't let the cross be the end!

Jesus said, "Take up your cross and follow me." The journey doesn't end at the cross! *The cross is where it begins.* The resurrected life of Christ began at the cross. Your resurrected life begins there as well.

Consider these verses:

> Our old sinful selves were crucified with Christ so that sin might lose its power in our lives. We are no longer slaves to sin.
>
> Romans 6:6 NLT

> I have been crucified with Christ and I no longer live, but Christ lives in me. The life I now live in the body, I live by faith in the Son of God, who loved me and gave himself for me.
>
> Galatians 2:20

The invitation to "take up your cross and follow me" is an invitation to live the resurrected life of Christ, free from the burden of sin, victorious over the devil, released from fleshly appetites, and in perfect unity with the Spirit of God.

When the trials of life knock you down . . . bear your cross.
When your heart aches and sorrow abounds . . . bear your cross.
When you come to the end of yourself . . . bear your cross.
When you find yourself clinging desperately to someone or something that seems out of God's control . . . bear your cross.
Die to doubt, defeat, discouragement, and despair at the cross, then rise to walk in the newness of life.

The Mind of Christ in You

Scripture teaches that you already have the mind of Christ. With these five steps you will get rid of the gunk that threatens to separate you from Him:

1. Choose to live a life of resistance.
2. Search for God in the dark places.
3. Confess your sins.
4. Focus on the facts.
5. Bear your cross.

In the Old Testament, God commanded the Israelites to keep the fire of the altar burning at all times (see Leviticus 6). The fire represented the presence and the power of God. With an incredible display of His glory, God lit the altar's fire (Leviticus 9:23–24). But He commanded the priests to keep that fire burning. It was their job to fuel the flame.

In the New Testament, the Spirit of God came to believers in "tongues of fire" (Acts 2). The Spirit of God brings His presence and His power. God lit the fire at Pentecost, but He commanded that we keep that fire burning. It is your job to fuel the flame.

Commit to these five steps and you will embrace the mind of Christ.

QUESTIONS TO CONSIDER

1. Which of these five steps challenges you the most?
2. Share a time when your faith was challenged and God proved himself faithful to His Word.
3. What does this statement mean to you? "The resurrected life of Christ began at the cross. Your resurrected life begins there as well."

Divine Power
to Destroy Strongholds

As you learn to live the resurrected life, you will learn to exercise the divine power God has given you to destroy strongholds. Paul urged believers in Corinth to use the weapons God gave them to demolish arguments and captivate thoughts:

> For though we live in the world, we do not wage war as the world does. The weapons we fight with are not the weapons of the world. On the contrary, they have divine power to demolish strongholds. We demolish arguments and every pretension that sets itself up against the knowledge of God, and we take captive every thought to make it obedient to Christ.
>
> 2 Corinthians 10:3–5

Let's examine these verses closely by listing the true statements they contain:

1. We live in the world, but we don't wage war the way the world wages war.

2. The weapons we use are not of this world.

3. Our weapons have divine power to demolish strongholds.

4. We destroy arguments and pretensions that arrogantly set themselves up against God.

5. We take captive every thought and make each one obedient to Christ.

So what are these divine weapons? In this chapter we will discuss their characteristics, then in the next three chapters I will identify three of them.

Characteristics of Divine Weapons

The weapons God has given you are supernatural and they have divine power. The weapons God has given you are spiritual, not physical. This is because the battle is spiritual, not physical. If you were fighting a physical battle, you would use physical weapons, such as swords and shields, guns and cannons, maybe even missiles. But because your war is spiritual, you use spiritual weapons. Spiritual weapons are custom designed to be effective in spiritual battles. Note what your spiritual weapons are able to do.

The weapons God has given you destroy strongholds. They destroy arguments and every proud obstacle raised up against the knowledge of God. The weapons God provides have the power not only to destroy but also to subdue. Whatever thoughts and arguments are not destroyed are made captive to the obedience of Christ.

What exactly are these arguments, pretensions, and strongholds? They are the weapons of the resistance. The arguments originate in worldly philosophy, theories, and ideas. They are logic, rationale, and reasoning. Pretensions are Satan's imitations and counterfeits that pretend to deliver what only God provides. They include the desires of the flesh and the passions that drive the human heart separated from Christ. These pretensions pretend to deliver pleasure, peace, satisfaction, and fulfillment. And for a brief season they seem to do just that, but they always lead to death.

Strongholds are the deeply entrenched arguments and pretensions that have grown more powerful through the ages. They have gained their power through their effectiveness in defying the advancement of the kingdom of God. Strongholds include pride, selfishness, offense, control, and fear. They all find their origin in unbelief.

We could go into great detail and name every argument, pretension, and stronghold we could imagine, but the truth of these verses is that no matter what the arguments are, we have been given the weapons to silence them. No matter how pretentious the pretensions might be, we have been given the power to destroy them. And no matter how strong the strongholds might seem, we have weapons made to demolish them.

The weapons God has given you have divine power. Think about this divine power. I drove an SUV that had a V-8 engine for a little while. I'm not sure what that means exactly, but I think it meant I could press the gas pedal and expect speed. That car had some powerful get-up-and-go! My V-8 engine was man-made, not divine. Man-made power still needs a source. My SUV ran on gasoline and oil and I'm sure other liquids I know nothing about.

All power on earth is generated by earthly elements, such as chemicals, water, wind, and fire. Power comes in all different forms. But the power that fuels the weapons you use in spiritual warfare comes from God himself. The Creator of chemicals, water, wind, and fire is the God who empowers your divine spiritual weapons. The weapons you've been given have divine power coming directly from God!

Consider the most amazing display of God's power that you can possibly imagine. Some things that might come to your mind are Niagara Falls, a hurricane, a volcano, a tsunami, or an earthquake.

I visited Pompeii on a trip to Italy and was overwhelmed when I realized the power of the sudden eruption of Mount Vesuvius in AD 79 that left people dead in their flight. Many people in surrounding areas believed they had been destroyed by the wrath of the gods. God's power as demonstrated in the force of nature is fierce.

The weapons you've been given have God's power. Their power is unsurpassed; these weapons bear the mark of the Maker. They have divine power to silence arguments, destroy pretensions, and demolish strongholds.

The Difference Between Divine and Supernatural

I am going to identify three of the many divine weapons you have to fight with. My hope is that by thoroughly identifying these three, you will learn how to identify many more. Invite God to reveal your spiritual arsenal to you as you armor up and fight your battles.

As a reminder, every spiritual soldier needs to be properly dressed and armed for battle. Although this book is not designed around the various elements of the spiritual battle armor, that armor is of utmost significance and importance. You can read the description of your spiritual battle attire in Ephesians 6:10–18.

The three weapons I will discuss in the next three chapters are:

1. The divine weapon of acceptance
2. The divine weapon of praise and thanksgiving
3. The divine weapon of intercession

I almost referred to these weapons as supernatural. But I decided to call them divine instead. Here is why: Supernatural refers to phenomena that supersede natural, or earthly, laws and realities. Supernatural powers belong to any spiritual being that operates beyond the laws of nature. The devil and his demons have supernatural powers. This is why other world religions experience wonders. Remember the Egyptian magicians who mim, miracles of God when Moses interacted with Pharaoh? Th recipients of the supernatural power of the gods of Egypt, _.I were demons that were cast out of heaven with Satan.

Divine weapons belong to the Divine Ruler over all heavenly powers. Divine weapons belong to the King of Kings and Lord of Lords. They are more powerful than supernatural weapons. They have divine power to annihilate the schemes, strategies, and even spiritual powers of all other principalities and rulers who try to destroy you. You have divine power to destroy.

The Key to Using Divine Weapons That Destroy Strongholds

The key to using these weapons is found at the very end of 2 Corinthians 10:5: "We take captive every thought to make it obedient to Christ."

Take captive every thought and make it obedient to Christ. Through your disciplined obedience to the lordship of Christ in your life, you release the powerful spiritual weapons that have divine power to demolish strongholds.

A great way to begin each day is to open your eyes while your head is still on your pillow and do these three things:

1. Declare the truth about your day: "This is the day the Lord has made. [I] will rejoice and be glad in it" (Psalm 118:24 NLT).
2. Think of ten reasons to thank God.
3. Declare Jesus Lord of your thoughts and profess aloud your intent to take authority over every thought this day.

If you do this, the minute you roll over and step out of bed, the demons will shudder and say, "Oh no, she's up!"

QUESTIONS TO CONSIDER

1. What does it mean to fight with spiritual weapons that have spiritual power?

2. What thoughts haunt you most? How might you take authority over those thoughts today?

3. How does knowing the power of your weapons impact you as you fight your battles?

(17)

The Divine Weapon of Acceptance

Because God is truth, He gives those who are His children the power to discern truth in all situations. Because we have the power to discern truth, we have the power to accept what is true, what is not true, what is real, and what is not real.

We have the power to accept the things we cannot change as well as the power to change the things we can. I'm sure you are familiar with the Serenity Prayer by Reinhold Niebuhr, but are you familiar with the entire prayer? I think I like the second verse better than the first! It says, "Accepting hardships as the pathway to peace; . . . trusting that He will make all things right if I surrender to His Will."

The key to wielding this weapon of acceptance is to have "the wisdom to know the difference." While God gives you the power to accept life as it is, He also expands your reality to embrace His possibilities. You live in a sin-stained world ruled by a master deceiver. Therefore, focus your attention on Jesus (the author and finisher of your faith) and trust that He will act (in response to your prayers) according to what He knows is best.

The best Scripture to support this weapon of acceptance is this:

> *Trust in the Lord* with all your heart
> and lean not on your own understanding;
> in all your ways submit to him,
> and he will make your paths straight.
> Proverbs 3:5–6 (emphasis mine)

Accept the Reality of God's Promises

We've discussed the power of God's Word throughout this book. And I want to discuss it again here. The weapon of acceptance includes standing firm on the promises of God. Let me describe for you the difference between letting God's promises comfort you in your trouble and releasing them to conquer your trouble.

God's Word is true whether you choose to believe it or not (John 17:17). God's Word is powerful whether you receive it or not (Hebrews 4:12). God's person and His purpose are revealed in His Word, and His plans will be accomplished (Job 42:2). God invites you to experience an intimate relationship with Him (John 1:12), and He is passionate about partnering with you in accomplishing His plans (Matthew 28:19). But He will be God, and His plans will be accomplished with or without you.

God's Word does all that it claims to do. The list of these claims would be extensive, but it includes correcting and training (2 Timothy 3:16), empowering (Romans 1:16), building up (Acts 20:32), giving success and prosperity (Jeremiah 29:11), providing direction (Psalm 119:105), and I could go on and on. However, the Word of God is powerless in your life until you choose to live under its authority. The power of God's Word is released through the will of His person. God accomplishes His Word in you when you choose to live in unity with Him. As you take God at His Word, follow His teaching, and honor His authority in your life, you release His promises so that they can be brought to reality in your life.

The promises of God released on the battlefield of your life are His rewards for the confidence you place in Him. In Hebrews we read, "Without faith it is impossible to please God, because anyone who comes to him must believe that he exists and that he rewards those who earnestly seek him" (Hebrews 11:6).

The promises of God are given freely to all of us (John 3:16). But they are released through men and women who choose to trust Him in their circumstances. God's promises are released by faith. When you use the divine weapon of acceptance, you release the power of God's promises in your life.

Hannah Accepted the Promise of God

Here is how this works. I, and every other woman who's dealt with infertility, love the story of Hannah when she poured her heart out before the Lord at Shiloh. Hannah's heart was overwhelmed with her longing for a child. Unless you've experienced infertility, you can hardly imagine her grief and her deep yearning. To make matters worse, Hannah had a heckler. The devil loves to assign some foolhardy soul the role of heckler. Peninnah had children, but she was jealous of Hannah because their husband loved Hannah more even though she hadn't produced any offspring. (Imagine having to share a husband with another woman!) Peninnah made fun of Hannah's infertility. The Scripture tells us that this went on "year after year" (1 Samuel 1:7).

You've been there and so have I. You go to the Lord in prayer, you beg again and again and again. You want peace in your home, restoration of your family, healing for your hurts, freedom from addictions, and nothing ever comes from those prayers. You agree with the writer of Proverbs 13:12, "Hope deferred makes the heart sick."

But Hannah had a breakthrough and so will you. One day when Hannah was praying, Eli heard her. At first, he joined the heckling.

"What a mess you are, woman! Stop your drinking!" (That's my paraphrase of 1 Samuel 1:14. I've always found it interesting that Eli rebuked Hannah so readily and yet seemed to disregard the sacrilegious practices of his own sons.)

Hannah quickly corrected Eli:

> "Oh no, sir!" she replied. "I haven't been drinking wine or anything stronger. But I am very discouraged, and I was pouring out my heart to the Lord. Don't think I am a wicked woman! For I have been praying out of great anguish and sorrow."
>
> "In that case," Eli said, "go in peace! May the God of Israel grant the request you have asked of him."
>
> "Oh, thank you, sir!" she exclaimed. Then she went back and began to eat again, and she was no longer sad.
>
> 1 Samuel 1:16–18 NLT

Hannah's story illustrates for us what happens in our lives when we release the promises of God. She could have easily responded to Eli, "You don't understand! I've been praying about this for years and God hasn't done anything."

She could have argued with Eli, she could have reasoned with Eli. Hannah could have resisted Eli's promise, but instead she received it. And because Hannah received the promise of God, she was no longer sad. Hannah was pregnant with the promise of God before she conceived the promise of God.

Hannah exercised the powerful weapon of acceptance and released the divine power of God in her life. Samuel was conceived, dedicated to the Lord, and surrendered to His purpose. He became a great partner with God in His unstoppable plans.

To exercise the powerful weapon of acceptance, recognize the hardships of this life as pathways to peace. Trust God to make all things right as you surrender to His will. And when God declares what He intends to do, become pregnant with his promise.

Has God given you His Word? Has He made you a promise?

If so, accept the reality of it. No need to keep on begging when the enemy heckles you. Boldly proclaim your promise aloud and shout, "Amen!" Let the promise of God be conceived in you and let it grow in the womb of your faith as you excitedly prepare for its arrival. That promise will come in the "fullness of time." Until then, God's got a very good reason for making you wait.

QUESTIONS TO CONSIDER

1. How can you know the truth? (Hint: Jesus said, "I tell you the truth" seventy-eight times. I've listed these verses at www. LeighannMcCoy.com/SpiritualWarfareTools.)

2. What might it look like if you were "taking this sinful world as it is, not as I would have it"?

3. What can you do to prepare for the arrival of your promise?

(18)

The Divine Weapon of Praise and Thanksgiving

Did you know that toxic thoughts in your brain actually affect your body the same way that physical injury does? According to Dr. Caroline Leaf, a cognitive neuroscientist with a PhD in communication pathology, specializing in neuropsychology (who is also a Christ follower), toxic thoughts trigger the release of the same protein in the liver that causes inflammation in the body. Too much inflammation in the body leads to mental and physical disorders.[1]

While we can't control the circumstances or people in our lives, we can control our reaction to them. Praise and thanksgiving combat toxic thoughts and work to keep balance in our lives. Consider these biblical instructions to thank and praise God:

> Give thanks in all circumstances; for this is God's will for you in Christ Jesus.
>
> 1 Thessalonians 5:18

> All this is for your benefit, so that the grace that is reaching more and more people may cause thanksgiving to overflow to the glory

of God. Therefore we do not lose heart. Though outwardly we are wasting away, yet inwardly we are being renewed day by day.

2 Corinthians 4:15–16

Give thanks to the Lord, for he is good; his love endures forever.

1 Chronicles 16:34

The Lord is my strength and my shield; my heart trusts in him, and he helps me. My heart leaps for joy, and with my song I praise him.

Psalm 28:7

Enter his gates with thanksgiving and his courts with praise; give thanks to him and praise his name.

Psalm 100:4

Does 1 Thessalonians 5:18 say to thank God in all things? Certainly Paul understood that there would be certain things that were exempt from thanksgiving. When I was diagnosed with cancer, my dear friend and prayer partner Kathleen brought me guacamole (because guacamole cures everything, even cancer). And along with the guacamole, she brought me a detestable little book titled *31 Days of Praise* by Ruth Myers.

I was kind of mad at my friend Kathleen. What was she thinking? If ever there was a time that I didn't want to praise, it was when I was diagnosed with cancer. But sweet, dear Kathleen assured me this little book was my pathway to joy even though my journey now involved cancer. So I read these words in the foreword of that book:

> *Thirty-one Days of Praise* is down to earth. It touches you where you live and walks where you plod. It is not a book that tells you to praise because "you are supposed to" and "you will be blessed" if you do. Rather it inspires and motivates you to praise from the heart.
>
> This book deals with the realities of living in a fallen world with its disappointing relationships, unfulfilled longings, and shattered dreams. It meets you where you are in the midst of your pain and

turmoil and enables you to see these things from a perspective that is true. As a result, even in the face of heartache, there is praise and the joy of a deeper intimacy with God. Praise itself becomes a blessing because it is real, and not just a rehearsal of words.[2]

When I reluctantly opened that little book and read those words, I was sold. I went through my thirty-one days in between surgery and recovery and discovered that Kathleen was right. This secret weapon has divine power to destroy the strongholds of despair, discouragement, depression, and doubt.

Praise and Thanksgiving Are the Expressions of Acceptance

Praise and thanksgiving go hand-in-hand with the divine weapon of acceptance.

Praise announces the truth about God. Praise declares the absolute truth that God is the same regardless of the circumstances (Hebrews 13:8), that His purposes are perfect (Psalm 33:11), and that His plans will not be thwarted (Job 42:2). Praise blasts the stronghold of doubt out of the way and advances you past the seemingly impenetrable walls that Satan builds with his minions assigned the task of pestering Christians with unbelief.

On the flip side, the absence of praise can give the powers of darkness unnecessary footing on territory that belongs to God. Watch your words; they reflect your heart. Your own words can either invite demonic forces of unbelief or scatter them. This morning I got out of bed and said, "I can't handle this anymore" in reference to the battle that is waging in my head and in my heart. Tom responded with this: "Oh yes you can. You must! You do not have a choice, and you will make it."

When I was going through chemo treatment, I wore a pack of powerful poison around my waist. It had a tube that connected with the port inserted in my body just below my left collarbone.

For forty-eight hours I heard the pump release toxic chemicals into my body. I knew those chemicals would cause me to be nauseous, they would deplete my energy, they would hinder my thought processes, and sometimes make me wish I were dead. I hated that poison. Of course, I knew it was necessary for fighting cancer, but I hated cancer too.

On most Sunday nights before the next round of chemo began, I cried like a whiny toddler and said to Tom, "I can't do this anymore." He'd look at me tenderly with tears in his eyes and say, "Leighann, it's hard, but it's not too hard."

There were many nights that I wore that pump with those words echoing through my mind. It was my song of praise. I know, I could have come up with a better song than that, but it was all I could muster. And those words were truth. It was hard, but it wasn't too hard, and today I am healthy and strong.

Praise is the declaration of truth about God in the face of circumstances crafted by Satan to discourage and defeat you.

Thanksgiving reminds you of how worthy God is of praise. As you remember what God has done in the past, you recognize that whatever He's yet to do in your present will be accomplished. It is simply a matter of time. Thanksgiving is like a compass reminding you of your spiritual bearings. Thanksgiving points you to your spiritual "true north."

God dwells beyond time and space. Your tomorrows are His yesterdays. Thanksgiving helps you remember this fact. When you wield your mighty weapon of thanksgiving, go ahead and place yourself with God in the heavenlies. Imagine your current battle already won. Imagine God's undeniable faithfulness to His promise. Thank Him for His sustaining power that kept you strong in the fight. Thank Him for the victory, the complete defeat of your enemy, and the spoils of victory that surprised you. Then, just for fun, go ahead and taunt the devil with your own imagination and declare God able to do "exceedingly abundantly beyond all you could ask or imagine" (see Ephesians 3:20).

This powerful weapon of praise and thanksgiving ushers you through heaven's gates and into God's courts of praise.

QUESTIONS TO CONSIDER

1. Can you think of anything you have trouble thanking God for?

2. When have you, or someone you've known, offered God a sacrifice of praise? What happened when you did?

3. Why are praise and thanksgiving so powerful in spiritual warfare?

19

The Divine Weapon
of Intercession

As I'm writing this book, I'm reading a collection of Andrew Murray's work. Andrew Murray was a preacher in the 1800s. After he retired, he wrote numerous books, most of them on the subject of prayer. Two of my favorites are *The Ministry of Intercession* and *With Christ in the School of Prayer*.

Andrew Murray has reminded me through his writings that God longs to demonstrate His power and His love on the platforms of our lives. When you intercede for your children, God is eager to hear and answer your prayers. You have heavenly power that you can pray down on others! Your prayers matter. They matter a lot.

In Ephesians 6, the strategy for warfare is simple: Once you get your armor on, pray.

I've already talked to you about the powerful prayer of relinquishment in chapter 8. Once you've completely and thoroughly relinquished your situation to God, every prayer you lift up has divine power to destroy strongholds. If you haven't waved the white flag of surrender and completely trusted God with your burden, the minute you do, all the prayers you've been offering will be released as God opens heaven's doors in response to your submission.

I am picturing what might happen if the Hoover Dam suddenly burst. Heaven's power is pressing at the seams, bulging with God's desire to be released on your turf if you will only give your heart completely to Him. As the classic hymn proclaims, "Oh, what peace we often forfeit. Oh, what needless pain we bear. All because we do not carry everything to God in prayer."[1]

Demons tremble when you pray. They've got no power whatsoever to defeat the flow of God's power when you position yourself as a conduit through which His purpose flows.

Big Hero 6 and the Power of Intercessory Prayer

In Big Hero 6, an animated movie I enjoyed with my granddaughter, the superhero (who was a confused teenager) created tiny little robots that were nothing more than seemingly innocent magnets. But when those tiny robots got together they became a powerful force. They were controlled by a mind sensor; whoever wore the sensor controlled the little robots. Well, you can imagine what happened. The mind sensor was stolen by the bad guy. So the superhero recruited some of his friends, and the six of them embarked on a mission to recover it. All the while they are set back by the army of tiny little robots.

First the superheroes tried to take the sensor off the villain's head, but after several humiliating failures, they realized that all they had to do to break the sensor's power was to separate the tiny robots from the villain. So they refocused their energy from removing the mind sensor off the villain to breaking the bond of the robots. And victory was won! Of course, my favorite line from the movie was this: "We didn't set out to be superheroes. But sometimes life doesn't go the way you planned."

Don't you love that? It's the way I feel about prayer and spiritual warfare. I didn't set out to be a prayer warrior, but sometimes life doesn't go the way you planned.

The point I want to make with *Big Hero 6* is that the superheroes broke the bond that held those tiny robots together and then they defeated their enemy. This principle of connection works in relationship to prayer and spiritual realities. Satan knows this truth, and we would do well to learn it too.

There is power in our unbroken connection with God. But when that connection is severed (by sin, the flesh, worldly affections, and prayerlessness), Satan (the villain) gains power over us to steal, kill, and destroy what is good in our lives. Likewise, prayer works in breaking free from the power Satan exercises over us! When we pray, we allow the Holy Spirit to break the bonds we have with the "hooks" the Enemy uses to detach us from God. And then we reattach ourselves to the real Mastermind of the universe and we are once again authoritative extensions of His power on earth!

Just remember, the power is not in us but in God. When we link ourselves to His mind, He will use us to accomplish things that would be impossible without Him. If you haven't seen *Big Hero 6*, go see it; you'll be glad you did.

When we position ourselves as intercessors, we become the passageway through which divine power releases from the throne of God in heaven and flows among us here on earth. Jesus yielded himself completely to God, and God's power coursed through Him. You could argue, "Well, of course it worked that way. Jesus is divine!" I would agree with that argument except that Jesus said, "I tell you the truth, anyone who believes in me will do the same works I have done, and even greater works, because I am going to be with the Father" (John 14:12 NLT).

Jesus intended that our intercession be active, not passive. Jesus said that the person of the Holy Spirit would release the same power that God released in Him while He was walking on the earth. The goal of our intercession is to be a conduit, a passageway, a "mind sensor" that connects the divine power of God to the hearts, heads, and lives of the people we love.

The goal of your intercession is to release the divine power of God that sets the captives free, opens the gates of iron, and breaks the chains of darkness in the lives of those we love. (See Isaiah 45:2.)

From the Courtroom to the Throne Room

A friend gave me a book written by a woman who urges her readers to imagine a heavenly courtroom where God is the judge, Jesus is the defense attorney, and Satan is the prosecutor.[2] Visualizing this heavenly court, I imagined a mother standing before God, representing her daughter, who was being brought to court by her fervent prayers.

As she prayed, I heard Satan bringing legitimate charge after charge against her dear child. With every charge the mother beseeched the Judge to refuse to hold her daughter's sins against her. She never made excuses and didn't expect Him to disregard them. Instead, she reminded Him that her daughter wouldn't even be living if He weren't on His throne. She reminded herself as she told Him that her child made a profession of faith at a very young age. She reminded Him also of the recommitment of her life that she made as a teen. Then the mother confessed that there was no way her daughter could understand the implications of her actions.

The mother cried out, "She's been tested and tried, and fell victim to the wicked schemes of the Enemy. The same could happen to me!"

Jesus stood silently beside her, and she looked longingly into His eyes. "Didn't you cry out from the cross, Lord, 'Father, forgive them, for they know not what they do!'? I assure you as her mother that if she knew you like I know you she couldn't possibly do the things she's done. If she really understood, she would bow before you, worship and adore you. Please bear with her a bit longer, draw her to yourself, and fulfill the promise you made to me many years ago when I first became concerned over the decisions she was making."

After that the mother wept. She lifted her hands in praise and then bowed before the throne. And as she worshiped, the accuser was dismissed.

With His dismissal, the Judge said, "Where is your accuser?"

The mother looked around and was immediately overwhelmed at the beauty of her surroundings. The sterile court room was gone and in its place was a glorious throne surrounded by brilliant gemstones. Twenty-four elders sat on twenty-four thrones. They were clothed in white and had gold crowns on their heads. In front of the throne was a shiny sea of glass, sparkling like crystal. Through praise and intercession the distraught mother had made the transition from the courtroom to the throne room. The accuser was gone, and she was now standing on holy ground.

Before the throne of God, this beautiful mother joined the voices of the heavenly hosts and cried out, "You are worthy, O Lord our God, to receive glory and honor and power. For you created all things, and they exist because you created them." (See Revelation 4 for a vivid description of the throne room of heaven.)

This is what happens when you join the mighty work of intercession.

Intercession, the Ultimate Plan of God

David Platt, president of the Southern Baptist Convention's International Mission Board and author of *Radical,* said this: "God judges sin. God provides a mediator. God supplies mercy."[3]

He was teaching from the story of Moses out of Exodus 32, when he interceded for the Israelites after they'd worshiped the golden calf. Moses' intercession rescued the children of Israel from the wrath of God. Platt went on to draw the parallel with Jesus, who paid sin's wages to become the ultimate mediator so that God's righteousness was satisfied and we could receive His mercy rather than His wrath.

God operates the same way today. His holiness reveals and rebukes sin. But before He unleashes His wrath, He sets mediators to stand between sin and himself.

Intercede for Your Family With Power

There are many ways to pray for those you love. The best way to present your requests before God is with complete honesty and total abandon. Your prayer posture should be one of humility, surrender, and confidence.

Ephesians 3:14–21 gives us a great scriptural pattern for interceding for our loved ones:

> For this reason I kneel before the Father, from whom every family in heaven and on earth derives its name. I pray that out of his glorious riches he may strengthen you with power through his Spirit in your inner being, so that Christ may dwell in your hearts through faith. And I pray that you, being rooted and established in love, may have power, together with all the Lord's holy people, to grasp how wide and long and deep is the love of Christ, and to know this love that surpasses knowledge—that you may be filled to the measure of all the fullness of God.
>
> Now to him who is able to do immeasurably more than all we ask or imagine, according to his power that is at work within us, to him be the glory in the church and in Christ Jesus throughout all generations, for ever and ever! Amen.

1. *Pray passionately.*

    Paul's prayer for the church at Ephesus was passionate. He fell to his knees and cried out to God.

2. *Pray bodaciously.*

    Paul asked God to heap His glorious riches on His friends. He asked that God strengthen them with power in their inner being. Only God can do that. The passions of the flesh, the empty promises of sin, can only work on a person from the outside in. God, on the other hand, has access to the hearts and minds of your loved ones. He can work from the inside out.

3. *Pray expectantly.*

Paul began to imagine what the answer to his prayer might look like. He prayed that once the believers were rooted and established in love, they would begin to understand the vastness of God's love. And then, that they would experience God's love in such a way that they might know by experience the marvelous love of God.

4. *Pray beyond your ability.*

Even after praying this passionate, bodacious, expectant prayer, Paul recognized that God could do more . . . much more. Pray knowing that whatever you ask, God is able to deliver so much more.

The main thing to remember when you pray is that God hears and answers your prayers.

Jesus Lives Today to Intercede for Us

Just as Jesus does for you, so you can do for your children. Because you've been redeemed by the blood of the Lamb, you can go before the throne of grace with boldness. You can intercede for your child's redemption and stand in the gap until he's saved. Consider these truths:

Let us then approach God's throne of grace with confidence, so that we may receive mercy and find grace to help us in our time of need.

Hebrews 4:16

I have posted watchmen on your walls, Jerusalem; they will never be silent day or night. You who call on the Lord, give yourselves no rest, and give him no rest till he establishes Jerusalem and makes her the praise of the earth.

Isaiah 62:6–7

Take full advantage of this powerful weapon of intercession! Approach the throne of grace with confidence and give Him no rest until He establishes you and your family.

QUESTIONS TO CONSIDER

1. Do you believe God is eager to hear and answer your prayers?
2. If you were in heaven's courts, what would you say when you stood before the Judge?
3. What is the difference between approaching God's throne of grace with uncertainty and approaching it with confidence?

PART 5

Protecting Your Children

Now, wiles is not a word we use a lot in our culture today. It means "organized conduct, plans of war or strategy or methodology." And I personally believe that Satan has a strategy for every one of us. He knows our weaknesses; he knows our strengths. And he will stop at nothing if he thinks he can victimize us for his own purposes.

—David Jeremiah, *Answers to Questions About Spiritual Warfare*

You Are Responsible for Your Family

Several years ago, I embraced a naïve understanding of God's willingness to protect my children from harm. I chose to believe that whatever I didn't do as a parent would be covered by what God would do as the perfect parent and therefore I didn't really have to worry too terribly much when my children veered off course.

I was wrong.

I thought this was childlike faith, but now I know it was spiritual laziness. I failed to recognize the reality and intensity of the spiritual war. My children had targets on their chests because of the mere fact that they had parents who served God, prayed, and dedicated them to Him when they were babies. And so do yours. We are fighting the greatest battle of all time. As parents we must take this combat seriously and train with intensity.

One of the first things you need to understand as a parent is that it is your responsibility to protect your children from spiritual attack. You are responsible for what comes in your house and what goes out of your house. You are responsible for the core values of your family. You are responsible for the spiritual education of your children, and you are the one God expects to stand in the gap between them and Him (as a conduit of His grace and mercy and love), and between them and the world (as a barrier that hinders the onslaught of Satan's attack).

This responsibility does not belong to the church, although the church will assist you in this mission.

This responsibility does not belong to your children's grandparents, although they will no doubt join you in prayer if they are believers, for your children are their greatest blessing.

This responsibility does not belong to the school or the government or extracurricular activities, although many teachers, government leaders, troop moms, and coaches make tremendous impacts on the lives of countless children daily.

The responsibility of protecting your children belongs to you. Say aloud,

> I am responsible for protecting my children from spiritual attack.

Joshua understood this position of responsibility when he declared, "As for me and my household, we will serve the Lord" (Joshua 24:15).

While this might seem overwhelming to you, it might also seem empowering! You've got control! You have authority; you've got the power!

Every Attack Brings the Opportunity for Blessing

Before I tell you how the Enemy launches his attack against your kids, let me remind you of this powerful truth: "Every attack from the Enemy brings with it a divine invitation from the sovereign hand of God to learn by experience what Love does."

I wrote this statement in *Spiritual Warfare for Women* and it has proven true. God is love and He proves His love on the battlefields of our lives. When the Enemy attacks you, look for what God's love wants to teach you. Don't be afraid of what you're about to learn. Be wise and prudent, alert and self-controlled. In these next few chapters, I'm going to discuss the Enemy's general strategy and greatest targets as related to each stage of your children's lives. If you recognize the Enemy's attack as I identify his strategies, invite Love to teach you what He can do.

There are many ways Satan attacks our homes. I could never provide you with an exhaustive list, but I'm going to share three ways he comes after your family in every stage of your child's life. The following chapters are focused on each of these life stages: preschoolers, elementary-age children, preteens, teenagers, and adults.

Before you skip to the chapter that addresses your child's life stage, let me remind you that this is a book on spiritual warfare, not parenting. There are many great parenting books on the market and I encourage you to take the time to read some of them. I am not a psychologist, nor am I a child development expert. I've worked with children for many years, I've taught children, and I've reared three, but I am a Bible teacher and truth seeker. My focus is on the areas of our children's lives that the Enemy targets for attack, and what we, as parents, can do to conquer him.

If your child is suffering from serious behavioral, psychological, or spiritual issues, consult qualified professionals. Doctors, psychologists, Christian counselors, and pastors are trained and skilled in delivering healing, and God works through people.

QUESTIONS TO CONSIDER

1. Have you ever been naïve about what God would and wouldn't do for you as a parent?
2. What does this statement mean to you? "The responsibility of protecting your children belongs to you."
3. How can you be certain of the love of God in the midst of any spiritual attack?

21

You Are Responsible for Your Preschoolers

I'll never forget the feeling I had when they discharged me from the hospital with my newborn baby girl. I wanted a manual, a how-to guide, or some sort of tutor who would go home with me to help me do everything right so that I didn't mess her up. But they sent me on my way with my tiny little bundle of joy strapped into a car seat, screaming all the way home. I sat next to her in the backseat of our little Nissan Stanza, Tom drove with one eye on the two of us in his rearview mirror, and we both wondered what we'd gotten ourselves into.

Thank goodness they don't stay babies for long. The preschool years are full of wonder if you have one preschooler at a time. If you have three in three years they are full of dirty laundry, spit up, and ear infections. I have to believe that you are a better parent than I am if you've got preschoolers and you're already concerned enough about their spiritual well-being to be reading this book. Let me assure you that God has an extra measure of protection that He uses to make up for the mistakes we make when our children are young. The best thing about young children is their resiliency. Praise God for that resiliency.

There are many ways Satan targets young children for attack. All over the world preschoolers suffer and die of preventable diseases caused by poverty. In Belize, mothers don't even give their babies names until their second birthday because of the high rate of infant mortality. The devil's heinous evil is rampant in the hearts of people who abuse small children, expose them to violence, or make them witnesses to the abuse of others. As spiritual warriors we cannot close our eyes and ears to these atrocities just because we have families of our own. When will we not have families to love? One of the best things you can do for your children is to demonstrate your love for God by loving those who are helpless in His world. Don't overextend yourself to the neglect of your family, but be aware and ready to respond to God's heart for children by connecting with ministries that seek to meet the needs of "those less fortunate than we." (My Papa Smith prayed for "those less fortunate than we" at every breakfast I ever shared with him.)

Here are three ways the Enemy might launch attacks on your preschoolers: through nightmares, through their developing imagination, and through premature exposure to the adult world. I will briefly describe each of these, then give you suggestions on how to fight off the enemy attack when it comes your way.

Nightmares

When my daughter Kaleigh was four, she began having nightmares. She'd wake up in the night tormented by her dreams. I have talked with other parents whose preschoolers have had similar experiences. Could these be enemy attacks?

Kaleigh had a special sensitivity to spiritual realities at a very young age. When she was even younger than four, she told me that she'd seen the streets of gold, and that if she got to heaven before I did, she and Jesus would wait for me to get there. I loved her childlike faith. When those dreams began, I wondered if they were spiritual attacks. I'm convinced today that they were. I think the forces of darkness were messing with Kaleigh because they recognized that she was chosen for special assignment in God's kingdom work and they wanted to introduce her to fear at a very young age.

Fight back. I sat with Kaleigh as she dozed off to sleep. We prayed and asked God to remove those bad dreams and to watch over her as she slept. We talked about Jesus and His angels. We imagined what they might be doing in heaven, and I painted visual pictures for Kaleigh so that those images would be the last things on her mind before she went to sleep. Kaleigh's nightmares ended.

I didn't get alarmed about these dreams; I got mad. I didn't get anxious; I got practical. I didn't worry about what they meant or how they might affect her fragile psyche; I prayed over her, sat with her, and trusted God.

Imagination

None of my children had imaginary friends, but my sister did. I can't remember her friend's name right now, but I do remember that she had one. I know some teachers suggest these friends might be personifications of demonic spirits. I don't think they are. Imaginary friends are pretend and most children understand the difference between what is real and what is pretend. Imaginary friends are as normal a part of a child's play as when she or he gives their dolls, stuffed animals, or action figures names and conversation.

Your preschooler's developing imagination is a part of God's creative work in her mind and heart. However, the devil might use your son or daughter's experiences with scary people or situations to torment them in their imagination, and this is when you teach them to reel in those imaginary thoughts and make them line up with the truth in God's Word.

Fight back. Preschoolers are not ready to take hold of the complex truths hidden in God's Word, but they can understand and accept basic truths. See a list of these basic spiritual truths in the article "Basic Truths for Preschoolers" online at www.Leighann McCoy.com/SpiritualWarfareTools. Don't assume that your preschooler will automatically learn these truths. You must teach them to him!

When my son, TJ, was four, I read through the Bible with him. Every night we sat together on the floor beside his bed and read. We didn't skip a thing. He loved it! And along the way I was able to teach him that the stories in God's Word were real while the stories in his picture books were sometimes pretend. The Bible is full of stories of adventure, and for young children with active imaginations, those stories come alive in their minds.

Another way you can fight the Enemy on behalf of your preschooler is to take her to a Bible-believing church with a quality preschool program. Find out what she is learning in her class and talk with her about her lessons. Satan will try to convince you that your preschooler isn't old enough to be affected by church attendance, but he is wrong. These are your child's formative years and foundations are being laid in his mind and heart. You only get to lay foundations once. All the rest of his life will be built on the foundations laid during the preschool years. Be responsible to make sure your preschooler has solid spiritual foundations by taking your child to church and reinforcing what he is learning at home.

Exposure to the Adult World

This might be the most vulnerable area in your preschooler's life. Don't forget that your preschooler is watching what you watch on television even when you think she's playing. Don't forget that she's listening to the conversations around her even when you think she's not.

I know children who've been exposed to more violence on television than I care to imagine. They cannot process what they've seen nor can they get those images out of their head. I was with a three-year-old when she said to me, "My Daddy was in a akident and he got out of the fire and chased the bad guys and killed them!"

Her "akident" sounded a whole lot like Grand Theft Auto to me. Her Daddy most likely was in a "akident" sitting on his sofa with earphones on his head and a game controller in his hand. He most likely did chase the "bad guys" and she was trying to process why he killed them. He might have thought he was spending quality time with his daughter. He didn't know that his entertainment became her obsession. When the game was over, he turned off the television and went to bed, never giving it a second thought. At the same time, she went to bed replaying the images of what she'd seen over and over again.

Don't forget that you are just as responsible for what goes into your preschooler's head as you are for what goes into her mouth. Be careful what your preschooler sees on television, hears in adult conversations, and glances at on your iPad, phone, and computer.

"Oh, be careful little eyes what you see!"

Fight back. Turn off the television or get reacquainted with preschool-friendly entertainment. Be careful even with preschool-friendly entertainment that you don't allow mysticism and secular worldviews to subtly creep in. There are many phone apps, books, movies, and games that teach biblical truths and encourage Scripture memory and Christian concepts. Download these and play them with your preschooler.

The next time you get in a heated argument with your spouse, look at your preschooler's face. See the damage your temper is doing to him. Save your heated discussions for after they go to bed, and be diligent to apply Ephesians 4:32 to the atmosphere of your home: "Be kind and compassionate to one another, forgiving each other, just as in Christ God forgave you."

Labeling and Assessments

As I was writing these ways that Satan attacks your preschooler, this fourth angle of attack came to my mind and I must include it, so you get a bonus in this chapter.

Our children's issues are identified at a very young age. While some of that is good, some of it is not. The devil plants seeds of doubt and despair in your heart and mind and in the heart and mind of your child with our society's obsession with labels and assessments.

Insecure parents suffer anxiety when their preschooler is labeled slow, quiet, shy, aggressive, disruptive, etc. When my daughter Mikel was five years old, she met a well-known radio personality. She was definitely not shy, and more than able to make her requests known to her dad. Just after meeting this man, she asked her father for cotton candy. (We were at a church-hosted carnival when Mikel met Mr. Radio Man.) With more candidness than I preferred, Mr. Radio declared her to be strong-willed. I decided then and there that I didn't like that man. In hindsight, he was spot-on with his assessment of my daughter, but I didn't want Mikel to live her life thinking she had to prove or overcome a label. I don't want your children to have to do that either.

Fight back. Don't ever forget, *you* are the expert on your child. You know him/her better than anyone else. God appointed you as his parent. Listen to what others tell you and pray for discernment. I know many parents who ignore what others see because they have inflated visions of their child's behavior. Critics can be your friends. But take those criticisms before the Lord and ask Him to show you how to parent your child with wisdom, discipline, and respect. Don't let assessments and labels hurl you into a place of defensive parenting driven by fear. Get help, seek counsel, but don't cower in fear.

Furthermore, don't accept someone else's label of your child. When the world starts labeling your children, keep reminding them that they get to choose the kind of person they want to be and that God has amazing plans for their lives.

Preschoolers and Spiritual Warfare

Thank God for His special protection over our young children. The best thing you can give your preschooler is your own growing personal relationship with God. The second best thing is a safe home where he or she feels secure. If you are married, the third best thing you can give your preschooler is a healthy marriage where you model love and kindness on a daily basis. You win the war when you trust God to do in you and through you what you could never do without Him.

QUESTIONS TO CONSIDER

1. How does your child's imagination help him/her to understand God?
2. What can you do to shield your preschooler from too much exposure to the adult world?
3. Which preschool-friendly programs do you think are best for your child?

You Are Responsible for Your School-Age Children

We hosted Boohoo Breakfasts for kindergarten parents when my children were young. And although I did shed tears on the first day of school *every* year my children went, deep down inside I was elated that we were moving forward. The elementary school years are really some of the best years of your life as a parent. But they can be challenging as well. No matter if your children are home-schooled, attend private Christian schools, or go to public schools, the devil will still find ways to target them for attack. Three of their most vulnerable spots are these: relationships with siblings and friends, self-image, and the secular worldview.

Relationships With Siblings and Friends

Your own precious children can cause damage to your own precious children, and the devil can dance on those conflicts. My mother was an only child and she never could understand why my sisters and I simply could not and would not get along with one another. I have to confess that my own parenting skills were often lacking in the area of refereeing sibling conflicts. One of my favorite sayings was this:

"I'm not as interested in who started it as I am in who finishes it." (And I hoped they didn't finish it with bodily contact.)

Another of my favorites:

"Someone needs to take the high road!" To which one of my children once exclaimed, "I'm tired of taking the high road, it's her turn. I'm going to take the low road this time."

And then there was this one that I used far too often:

"I'm sure he didn't mean to. It'll be okay," which translated, "I don't really care right now."

I had a friend whose mother had some better ones than these:

"Be sweet or be beat!" and "Shape up or ship out!"

Siblings are great teachers. They teach your children how to deal with difficult people; they teach them how to get over offenses and resist the urge to hold grudges; and they teach them the world doesn't revolve around them. (Unless they are the baby of the family, and then they learn that it does indeed revolve around them.) In my home, we just gave in to our children's accusations that the "other child" was the favorite. They'd accuse us of playing favorites and we'd simply agree.

"You are right, [the other child] is my favorite." End of story.

But not only will the devil dance on sibling relationships, he will also take advantage of your children's relationships with their friends. While you can control what your children are exposed to in your own home, you cannot control what they are exposed to in your neighbor's home. Be careful where you let your children play and with whom they play. Be attentive to the way your child interacts with his friends. Is he a victim or a follower? Is he a bully? Is he a leader? Does he build up and encourage or tear down and tease? Host your children's friends in your home so that you can be aware of their relationships with one another.

Fight back. Concerning your children's relationships with one another, don't be lazy in pursuing peace in your home. It does matter if your children bully one another. Don't expect the more compliant child to always take the high road. Work to teach your children how to treat one another fairly, and insist that they exercise other-centeredness in your home. Be patient, be firm, but don't be lazy.

Regarding your children's relationships with other children, don't shrink back from monitoring your children's friends. Help your children identify other children who can be good friends. Help them know how to avoid those who are not. Teach your child that their friends influence them and that they influence their friends. When they have fallouts and misunderstandings, walk them through what happened and help them to learn from those experiences. Make sure your child has friends, and then demonstrate healthy friendships by letting them see you interacting with your friends.

When Kaleigh was in the first grade, she had a classmate who always made fun of her. She'd come home in tears recounting the ways he'd teased her. I suggested one afternoon that she ask him to stop. She called his number, asked to speak to him, and simply said, "Will you please stop teasing me?" He said, "Sure!" and that was the end of that. Kaleigh learned to address her troubles directly and she's practiced that consistently since then.

Not every difficult relationship is a direct enemy attack, but every difficult relationship does give you the opportunity to teach your child how to respond to others in Christlike humility while maintaining self-respect, in kindness while establishing boundaries, and in compassion and love while making wise decisions. All of these lessons pave the way for them to fight and win spiritual attacks throughout their lives.

Self-Image

By this stage of life, children begin to notice how they are different from one another. Some are short, some tall; others are thin or thick, pretty or plain. In their world these differences matter—a lot. The devil definitely works to create self-consciousness in your child's mind and heart as her body grows. Even if she doesn't mention it, know that she's analyzing her appearance and she notices the changes. What others say penetrates her heart. What you say penetrates her heart. If you're always talking about losing weight, she wonders if she needs to lose weight. If you don't like the way you look, she'll wonder how she looks.

Fight back. Talk with your child about his body. Help him to understand what to expect as he continues to grow. Be diligent to establish healthy habits. My children watched me exercise consistently. They knew that exercise was important to me. We ate healthy foods. When I was diagnosed with cancer, my fifteen-year-old son said, "Go figure! We didn't eat Ding Dongs growing up and you still got cancer!" Today my children are young adults and all of them are pursuing healthy lifestyles.

Find activities and interests that are age- and body-appropriate. Let your child know how beautiful they are, and help them develop the kind of self-image that David had when he proclaimed, "I am fearfully and wonderfully made; your works are wonderful, I know that full well" (Psalm 139:14).

I never let my girls call themselves fat. They were larger than some of their friends. I've yet to understand how children can grow up so skinny. When I was a child, the department stores had special sizing for kids like me. They called them "chubbies." But during that stage of my daughters' lives, I told them I'd let them refer to themselves as "fluffy" but never fat. Kaleigh reminded me the other day that I told them to say, "I am loved" each time they were tempted to say, "I am fat."

We laughed together and I cried out to God alone in prayer. I begged Him to help me help my girls to accept their bodies as marvelous machines and not to be hindered by obesity and the self-consciousness that often accompanies weight issues and causes people to isolate themselves from others. I asked God to do whatever He would to make sure that my girls grew up fulfilling the great purpose He had for their lives. I'll be honest with you and tell you that I also begged Him to make them thinner. He gave me a promise when I prayed that prayer. Perhaps you can cling to it today. Psalm 144:12: "Then our sons in their youth will be like well-nurtured plants, and our daughters will be like pillars carved to adorn a palace."

I also packed nutritious school lunches for them.

Secular Worldview

Unless you are actively engaged in teaching your child a Christian worldview, he or she will develop a secular worldview. Even if you take them to church, that one hour on Sunday morning (or even three hours a week) is not enough to counterbalance the ongoing steady flow of secularism that is coming at your children from all directions.

Fight back. Now is a good time to decide what you want to do about this. A good starting place is to host family devotions. I'll never forget how my father did this for us. Every morning my mother cooked breakfast and we ate that meal together as a family before we went to school. Over breakfast, my father read from a devotional book and led our family in prayer. That one practice probably made a bigger difference in my life than I've ever recognized. And you can do that *now*.

Turn off the television. Sit at the table together and share some meals as a family! If you don't, you'll wish you had. I cannot help but believe that countless battles could be won over bacon and eggs or chicken and rice if families would just eat and pray together.

I have many regrets as a parent, but one of the biggest ones is our lack of commitment to sharing meals together. If I had it to do over again, I would serve my family supper at the dinner table every night of the week (except Wednesday, when we are at church). I wouldn't feed them fast food on the way home from the ball field, and we wouldn't eat our meals on the run.

Consider your own value system and ask God if it honors Him. This is a good time to create your family's core values. I've provided a worksheet for this activity: "Developing Your Family's Core Values" at www.LeighannMcCoy.com/SpiritualWarfareTools.

Children and Spiritual Warfare

This is the season of your life as a family when you are most able to establish routines and habits. What might seem small and insignificant today will be the making of the memories that your children refer to eventually as the "good old days." This is your turn to make your family what you want it to be. But don't think, *I'll do that in a while,* for in a while your children will be grown.

Be responsible for your time, your menu, your agenda, and your goals. If you don't take responsibility for these, the world will, and the prince of this world is out to destroy you.

QUESTIONS TO CONSIDER

1. Are your children kind to one another? Do they treat each other fairly?
2. What can you do to foster your child's healthy self-image?
3. What are you doing to help your children develop a Christian worldview?

Be Responsible
for Your Preteens

Note that the title of this chapter is "Be Responsible for Your Preteens." Too many parents are tempted to shrink back as their children enter the most treacherous part of their journey toward adulthood. Don't do that! Be responsible for your preteen!

I jokingly say that middle school is just to be survived. The sixth, seventh, and eighth grades are amazing and horrible at the same time. Changes are happening at warp speed, and children in our culture are leaving fairly innocent childhoods behind and preparing to embark on the most dangerous part of their journey toward adulthood: their teenage years. The devil definitely prowls about the hallways of middle schools.

The good news is that many children who are reared in Christ-centered homes begin to make sense of their faith during this time. They begin to put the basic truths they were taught as children to task and look for the reality of God in their lives. Because their minds are starting to process abstract thoughts, they are ready to wrestle with deeper truths and concepts like lordship and forgiveness and long-suffering and surrender.

You have a great responsibility in guiding your son or daughter through the preteen years. Here are three areas where your preteen might be vulnerable to the enemy's attack.

Sex

Already?!

Yes, I'm sorry, but the truth is that children as young as eleven and twelve are sexually active. Sexting, oral sex, and pornography are all on the rise among preteen children. In our community, an eighth-grade girl and several boys were charged with child prostitution and pornography because she sent a text of her topless self to one boy who then shared it with others.

Sexual immorality is at the top of numerous sin lists in Scripture because it is so powerful in its appeal to the flesh, and it is so destructive to the hearts and minds of those involved in it. Sex is a powerful thing, and the devil knows it. He will do what he can to get your child all mixed up in sex as young as possible so that he can confuse her/his mind about many other things. Like many other powerful yet delightful experiences, sex is incredible as long as it is practiced within its God-ordained boundaries. Sex outside of God's parameters is destructive. Sexual immorality opens a floodgate of confusion, deception, and distortion in relationships.

If the devil can mess with your child's sexual identity, he will. If he can mess with your child's purity, he will. The devil is dancing in X-rated fashion and he begins his dance in middle school.

Fight back. First, take a deep breath and release that fear. Say aloud, "Greater is he that is in you, than he that is in the world" (1 John 4:4 KJV).

Now be smart!

Stay aware of what is going on in your preteen's world. Adjust your schedule to fit in time to be in his or her world. If she enjoys macaroni and cheese, make a game out of discovering how many places you can eat macaroni and cheese together. If he likes gadgets, hang out at the gadget store and learn about gadgets. As you discover and share in your child's world of interest, he will let his barriers down and begin to talk to you about the things that are going on there.

I watched all eighteen hours (it seemed) of *The Lord of the Rings* trilogy while traveling when my son was fourteen. Was I interested in *The Lord of the Rings*? No. Was my son? Yes. Was I interested in my son? Yes. Did I watch those movies? Yes. I chose to dive headfirst into his world because I didn't want him to fall prey to the Enemy's ability to create a void and then offer a way to fulfill it.

One of the best places I found for discovering what was going on in my children's worlds was behind the steering wheel of my car. Pile your car full of your children's friends and take them wherever they want to go. They will forget you are there and you will learn a boatload of information about what is going on in their lives.

Pray. Pray for your preteen's protection. He is entering a stage of life where you cannot protect him from every evil thing that might come his way. Pray that God will go where you cannot. And be attentive to where those places might be. Join other parents and pray from now until these children turn thirty. By then you might have grandchildren to pray for and your knees will be calloused enough to continue praying on them.

Teach your child about sex. Somebody's teaching them, and you might as well let your voice be the loudest in their heads. Don't shrink back, jump in and go for it. There are lots of great resources for you to use to take the lead in your child's sex education. I've included several of them in the article "Sex Education Tools for Parents." You can access this article at www.LeighannMcCoy.com /SpiritualWarfareTools.

Personal Electronic Devices

Most parents purchase their children their first personal electronic devices at this age. While PED's are great for keeping in touch with your children, they are also one of the devil's favorite places to hide. We have had the privilege of partnering with the local police department in our community to educate parents on the dangers that lurk in the seemingly innocent cell phone.

The fact is that middle schoolers know more about those things than their parents do. They know how to access anything and how to cover up much of what they've accessed. When you give your preteen a cell phone, you have given them keys to a world of privacy and responsibility. If you don't create accountability, you have given your child a tool just as dangerous as a pistol or a viper. The cell phone creates as much frenzy in the spiritual battle today as the Israelites did when they worshiped the golden calf in the desert.

"They put a cell phone in my hand, and voilà! Out popped this pornography, or intimate conversation, or sexting, or bullying, or . . . !!!"

Fight back. The bottom line is that you, the parent, are responsible for what happens with that PED. Don't think that just because your child knows what you expect of him, he will do it. Don't be naïve, and don't be paranoid. Find a happy medium and call it responsible.

Require your child to turn in his phone to you nightly. Charge the phone in your own room. Check the phone and stay on top of what he's accessing and what conversations he's having. Let your child know that his business is your business on that phone. Warn your child of the dangers of building relationships primarily through text and encourage her to continue talking to friends face-to-face.

Put all PED's in a basket at family dinnertime. Live without the phones so that you can tune in to one another. Start out with these rules and keep them throughout your child's teen years. Be surprised; be flabbergasted, in fact, if he or she suggests your rules are outrageous. You pay the bill!

Sports

What I'm about to say is going to be controversial. But I'm going to say it anyway. Sports teach our children many great things: teamwork, healthy competition, fairness, unfairness, how to win, how to lose, and the rewards of hard work. And sports in moderation are a healthy part of most every American child's life.

But at this age, sports can slip from moderation to excess.

I'll never forget when my girls were chosen for the All-Star softball team. We got to the athletic complex Saturday morning and were bombarded by team banners, speaker systems, manicured ball fields, and professional umpires. The uniforms the children were wearing looked like their mothers had ironed them. Welcome to the world of serious ball. I'd never seen anything like it, and to be quite honest, I was a bit overwhelmed.

We played our tournament and had our fun. And then within two years my own daughter was a member of one of the best girls' traveling softball teams Middle Tennessee had ever had. (No, I didn't press her uniform.) We were bit by the travel sports bug and off we went. It was fun, we all learned a lot, there were moments that were incredible, and the memories of them will last us a lifetime. But the day after my daughter left home to move into an apartment with her boyfriend (two weeks after she graduated from high school), I put all those trophies in a cardboard box and shoved them into the attic.

I didn't want to see them anymore. We spent all of those years playing ball when we could have been eating dinners together as a family, or participating in mission trips, or attending church camps, or camping, or skiing, or talking, or doing anything but sitting on bleachers watching our girls play ball.

Was it worth it? No.

Would I do it again? No.

The price we paid was higher than we knew at the time. Our other two children were left home alone, or spent their Saturdays in the ball-field dirt, and often didn't get to do the things they wanted to do because our weekends revolved around their sister's games. Our ball player got pretty good at hitting and playing center field. But she worked hard for that, and she always felt like she had to fight for her spot because there would always be someone who could take her place. The pressure was enormous, more than I think teenagers should be expected to manage.

When my son was in middle school he longed to be a basketball player. Basketball was the most popular sport at Heritage Middle School, and the atmosphere of the gym on game night was thick with energy. TJ made the middle school team, but had to work his tail off to get even two minutes of game time. He got his dad and me up at 4:45 a.m. to take him to the rec center where he could shoot one hundred free throws before school. He played club ball in between school seasons and went to camps in the summer. TJ ran and dribbled and shot and played and played and played. Finally, in the ninth grade, TJ gave up on basketball.

After all his hard work, he never could get more than a minute or so of game time. He was devastated, and I thought the devil had danced on my son's otherwise optimistic outlook on life, and permanently replaced his optimism with defeat through the demon of basketball. TJ bemoaned his hard work and declared that the only thing he ever learned from his basketball experience was that he could give his best and it would never be good enough.

But within a year TJ found a new interest. He decided that his "thing" was people. He read *How to Win Friends and Influence People* by Dale Carnegie and put the book to the test. When the principles of that book proved true in the halls of Independence High School, TJ discovered a whole new world of possibility. When he graduated from high school he was president of the student body. Today he speaks at middle school graduations and tells rising high school freshmen that what they choose not to do is just as important as what they choose to do. TJ encourages them not to be afraid to quit.

Fight back. I'm spending a little more time on this subject because I have a little more personal experience with it. My advice to you is to make sure that if your child is good at sports, he or she keeps the game in its proper place. I have a sweet friend who is training this summer at the Olympic Training Center in Colorado. She's had to sacrifice much for her sport, but she's maintained a Christ-centered focus and prayerfully followed God when she made the hard choices. I'm not against children playing sports. I am against sports playing our kids. As parents it's our responsibility to help our children find what they're good at and do it. But in the doing, we need to make sure they don't allow what they *do* to determine who they *are*.

Your child is more than the games they play, so much more. And even if they spend many hours in the gym or on the field, they still need help balancing their spiritual development, church activities, and family time. You are the one who will help them with these things.

If you do choose to play traveling ball, be intentional in taking Jesus into that world with you. My daughter's traveling ball coaches did an incredible job of this. They taught our girls to pray and to play together. When their games allowed them, they attended church services on Sunday mornings in whatever town they were playing. When their games didn't allow them to attend church, they took turns sharing devotions. We know several ball coaches who use their sport to share Jesus with parents and players.

Preteens and Spiritual Warfare

By this age your child can begin to understand deeper spiritual concepts. Talk to him about the truths in this book. Be aware of his level of understanding. Ask lots of questions and let her know that you are safe, trustworthy, and interested in what she's going through and what she's learning.

Talk about spiritual things. Don't ever stop and don't make it a big to-do. Just talk about spiritual things the same way you talk about other things. And by all means keep doing fun things together as a family. Good times together win spiritual wars!

QUESTIONS TO CONSIDER

1. What does your child know about sex?
2. What can you do to help your child be safe with his PED?
3. How can you help your child maintain a healthy balance in his life?

24

Be Responsible
for Your Teenagers

Note the title of this chapter as well: "Be Responsible for Your Teenagers." Even though your teens might not want you to be involved in their lives, you are and need to be. Take responsibility for them!

My husband and I shared dinner last night on the porch of our eighty-year-old farmhouse in the North Carolina mountains, otherwise known as my "laughing place." I told him that I'd really like to meet the twenty-five-year-old me. I wish that she and he (at twenty-five) could sit with us at dinner and we could share that meal together. I then imagined twenty-five-year-old Leighann sitting there with me, and I told her this:

> Don't work so hard at getting pregnant. Those children are not as much fun as you think they'll be. Sure, they're amazing and you'll love them like no other, but they are going to challenge you more than you can possibly know. They're going to break your heart and cause you to doubt God like you won't believe.

I've also said that I want to go to the hospital to greet new parents and say, "I am so sorry" instead of "Congratulations!"

I guess I'm being a bit melodramatic, but honestly, teenagers are scary. I always thought they were, and even though I've survived them in my home, I still think they're scary. When God wanted to scare the living daylights out of lukewarm parents, He allowed their children to become teenagers.

I heard on the radio that the freedom of the teenage years is a relatively modern phenomenon. It didn't come into existence until the 1950s, when children no longer worked as apprentices, but rather had more time and resources to play! Think about it. At what stage of life do you have more privileges than you have responsibility?

Privilege without responsibility is the perfect recipe for an enemy attack. And oh, how Satan loves to hang out with teens. He's more dedicated to students than most of our churches are. But don't think it's the church's responsibility to win spiritual battles for your teen.

It's yours.

Here are the areas in our teenagers' lives that are most vulnerable to attack: peer pressure, increased freedom, and the media. Of course, the areas of vulnerability that hit them as preteens continue during the teenage years as well.

Peer Pressure

While preschoolers and young children want to please their parents, teenagers want to please their friends. Peer pressure actually begins much younger than the teen years, but it makes its way to the front when your child hits this age. It's not unusual for you to be not so important anymore, and for your child's friends to be ever so important now. That's a scary thought when you think how they are ready to tackle the world with their twenty-eight years (two fourteen-year-old brains put together) of cumulative wisdom and experience.

Peer pressure can be good. The right friends will help draw out strengths in one another; they will fuel passions to change the world and encourage each other to grow.

Peer pressure can also be bad. The wrong friends will help expose weaknesses. They will fuel temptations and rob your child of God's best for his life.

I have a friend whose son was devastated by his father's addictions. He asked an adult friend how he could know if he had the same bent. He was terrified of living life like his father. The wise friend advised the young man to steer clear of all alcohol and drugs. That was the best way to avoid his father's demise. However, this same young man went to a party with friends. Someone encouraged him to take a drink, and accustomed as he was to being the life of the party, everyone was pleased when he played along. He was fourteen then. Today he is nineteen and steeped in addiction. His mother is constantly on her knees interceding for his release from Satan's hold.

Fight back. Peer pressure gains its power from the fear of being alone. Your teenager is growing away from the small world of home and making his way into the great beyond. As he goes, he experiences loneliness. No one likes to feel lonely. She searches for someone besides Mom and Dad to validate her, to value her, and to fulfill her need for significance.

You know that only God can do that, but she doesn't. Neither does he.

So what can you do? You can give yourself a pep rally. Say these things:

"I am still the parent!"

"Hoorah!"

"I have the power of the purse strings!"

"Hoorah!"

"I will be my child's mom/dad, not his/her friend!"

"Hoorah!"

Make pom-poms if you need to.

Keep your teenager involved in activities that attract healthy teens. Look for ministries that offer your teenager the chance to serve people from other socioeconomic classes. Find ministries that offer outrageously fun events that draw kids for the sheer fun and adventure of it. If your church doesn't have ministries like these, help start them or find a church that does. If your child is unhappy at church, take the time to discover why. Get involved in the student ministry and be a part of the solution. Encourage your teen to take their friends with them to church, and host wholesome fun in your own home.

When Kaleigh was in high school we hosted float building at our house. We have great memories of those crazy four weeks (one each year of high school). Not only did her classmates consistently build winning floats, but they also worked together across the typical extracurricular activity boundaries and had some good, safe fun. I also discovered that I'm allergic to tissue paper!

Rally with other parents and determine together that the God you serve is greater than the influence of your child's friends. Help to bear the burden of Satan's attacks. I was in a small-group Bible study with other parents of teens when my children were navigating adolescence. Together we commiserated, fasted, and prayed for God's power and provision in our children's lives.

Increased Freedom

With increased freedom comes increased opportunity to make some major mistakes. Your teenager will most likely make some major mistakes. Don't be surprised by this. Sometimes those mistakes might even offer some comic relief. At other times they will just about kill you. They can be devastating and disastrous. The important thing to remember is that as freedom increases, mistakes will happen, and God still reigns.

My son was mad, so he drove far too fast on the way home from the airport. I knew he was mad, but I feared for our safety, so I said, "Son, if you don't slow down, you're going to get a ticket." He was going about 60 in a 40 MPH speed zone. We made it home just fine that night, but the next night I tried to sleep knowing he was still out, and his curfew had passed. As I lay in my bed, I heard him come in and thanked God for bringing him home safely. He came up to my room and sat down on the floor beside my bed. He wasn't angry, but he did seem a bit uncharacteristically humble.

"Mom, you know how you said I was going to get a ticket?"

With increased freedom comes increased opportunity to make poor decisions. And when poor decisions are made, they come with consequences. Thankfully, TJ's consequence could be taken care of with some hard-earned cash. There are other poor decisions that result in much greater burdens. As I write this, I am in a texting relationship with a beautiful high school senior who's about to have a baby. She's confided in me that she often feels scared and alone. While her baby is going to be precious and God has great plans for his life, the challenge of rearing him is going to be hard, and she's going to miss out on a whole lot of life that she could have enjoyed had she made different choices. Her consequences are much more costly than those my son had to endure in traffic court.

Fight back. A natural part of growing up is an increase in independence and freedom. The irony of this is that with God our greatest place of maturity is in our dependence on Him, not our independence from Him. As your teenager exercises his newfound freedom, consistently remind him that even when you are not around, God is. Keep telling him that there are blessings in obedience and curses in disobedience. Both obedience and disobedience deliver consequences.

When she makes poor choices, hang on for the long haul. Invite God to use those experiences to teach her what she could never have learned any other way. Ask Him not to waste a single hurt. Don't shrink back from the responsibility and privilege you have to administer consequences that will encourage her to choose more wisely in the future.

Take time to talk about these things. Keep the lines of communication open by making time to be together. Don't schedule your conversations, but be intentional about talking when you are together. If you've been praying for your child all his life, double the time you pray for him now. He and you both need those prayers.

Media

This is a battle that has been fought for years. Now it's our turn to fight on behalf of our kids. We will blink twice and it will be their turn to fight for theirs. Pay attention to what your child is listening to! When my daughter's radio station went from Christian to country to ridiculous rap my husband knew something was up. His intuition was spot-on.

Pay attention also to what your children are reading. The devil is lurking in *Fifty Shades of Grey* and vampire stories, and even seemingly innocent romantic fiction. He's also making pornography more readily available than ever before. Be careful that your child doesn't escape to the world of reading and miss out on the real world of people. Collect the personal electronic devices and take a look at what they are doing there. The advancement of technology has allowed Satan to infiltrate our homes undetected. Don't let him do that. Insist that your children turn in their phones at night and give you their passcodes. Check their devices often and address what you discover there.

Films will always present temptations for teens. Know what your child is watching and don't forget that you can still say no.

Fight back. Some parents assume that since their teen doesn't want to hear them, they have to stop talking.

Pishposh!!

You have the responsibility to instruct your child whether or not he wants to hear you.

One of the things I said to my teens often was this: "Garbage in, garbage out." I warned them that their minds and hearts were just as affected by junk media as their stomachs and bodies were affected by junk food.

One of the greatest things my husband ever did for my son was to give him a book and challenge him to read it. *The Traveler's Gift* by Andy Andrews opened up a world of possibility for TJ. He's a voracious reader today of quality books. Another thing Tom did was help TJ set up lunch appointments with successful businessmen. At these lunches, TJ learned to listen, to ask good questions, and to grow in his relationship skills while gathering valuable insight from men who were older, wiser, and more accomplished than he.

The best way to defeat the effects of worldly and demonic media on your children is to keep the family unit intact by doing fun things together. Don't do what you did when they were five, but do what they find fun now. Invest your time and energy into activities that put watching a terrible movie or reading a trashy novel or listening to nonsense to shame. I've provided you with some ideas for fun things to do with your teens: "Fun Things for Families of Teens to Do Together" online at www.LeighannMcCoy.com/SpiritualWarfare Tools. But you know your family best. Continue the adventure of doing life together by embracing the activities that you all can enjoy.

Teenagers and Spiritual Warfare

Consider teaching your teenagers the truths in this book. Invite them to read a chapter and discuss it together. Ask them what they think and listen closely. Keep talking to your teen. Find ways to spend time together and be aware of how busy your family is. Slow down the pace if necessary! You'll be glad you did.

QUESTIONS TO CONSIDER

1. How have your child's friends helped/hindered her?
2. How much freedom is too much freedom for your son/daughter?
3. What can you do to monitor what media your child consumes?

25

Stay Alert
for Your Adult Children

Notice that the title of this chapter changed from the others. No longer are you responsible for your child. Isn't that great? But you're still their parent and your heart doesn't always experience the freedom your mind knows belongs to you. Even without the responsibility, parenting is not just an eighteen-year commitment.

It's a lifetime sentence with no parole!

But with that come the most delightful surprises—grandchildren!

If you're a parent of adult children, you most likely survived the teens. Now you are on the long-term journey of parenting adults.

Who knew this was a thing? Right?

I had no clue my parents were still parenting me until I found myself here. And then, lo and behold, I discovered they were. Just a few weeks ago, my mom and dad came with me to my "laughing place." While we spent the week together I wrote the first few chapters of this book. I didn't think much of it, but each of my now-adult children called me at least once daily, sometimes more. Though they distracted me from my writing, I enjoyed talking with them and did my part to listen and offer encouragement on the various issues they were bringing to me.

At the end of the week, my dad said, "Leighann, you are a good mother."

I was surprised at how much that meant to me. He went on to tell me that he was impressed with the way my children called me and the conversations we'd had even though he'd only heard them from my side of the phone.

Here I am, parenting my adult children and being parented by my own father. I am being blessed as I bless. We never grow too old to be parents or to be parented.

But our role as parents definitely changes. Adult children release us from having to be directors of their lives. Some adult children ease us out of our director's chairs while others topple us on our backsides and leave us lying all sprawled out on the ground with our feet stuck up in the air. Nevertheless, we are dismissed from the director's role.

So what do we do now? We become investors, advisors, critics, cheerleaders, and sometimes stagehands. I love most all of these roles, but often get them confused. Sometimes I critique when I should be cheerleading, and at other times I invest when I should just move some junk off the stage. I'm approaching this season of parenting as I approached the others, with my eyes wide open, my jaw dropping, and my knees bent.

Adult children experience the Enemy's attack the same way you and I experience his attack. Most likely the areas in your life that are most vulnerable will be the same areas your children find most vulnerable. The advantage in this season of your battle is that as your children mature, they rediscover how amazing you are! The disadvantage is that you have no control whatsoever over the decisions they make. All you can do is decide how you will respond to them.

Family First

When my children were born, my father recorded a message for them on cassette tape. He gave them a tape player and their cassettes on their sixteenth birthdays. A few weeks ago, just before my sister died of cancer, my daughter Kaleigh found her tape player and cassette. While she and I were cleaning out the clutter in my bedroom, we listened to PopPop's voice as he told us about the day Kaleigh was born. Kaleigh's twenty-one now, but as my father's voice filled my ears, I remembered her birth as if it were yesterday. He told us what was going on in the world, all over the world, which I thought was interesting because Kaleigh has a keen interest in global events. He then told her about her family, her ancestors and relatives she would never know. I was struck by my father's affection for family. Many times he mentioned that she had a great family and that there wasn't much in the world more important than family.

For my dad, family mattered. When my sister died, I realized how much family mattered to her. She never married and she didn't have any children of her own, so her family was my family of origin. I mattered to her as did my other two sisters. My parents mattered a lot! And so did my aunts and uncles and cousins. They all came to her funeral, but I hadn't seen many of them in many years. And that made me sad.

As parents of adult children, it will most likely be up to you to carry the banner of family for your kids. One of the best ways you can win against Satan's attacks on their lives is to continually remind them of their family heritage, of the values they learned when they were young, and of the faith you modeled before them.

Let your adult kids know when you are proud of them. They could be fiftysomething and still be thrilled to hear you compliment them.

Let them know that you will always be there for them no matter what comes their way. Don't forget that "love covers over a multitude of sins" (1 Peter 4:8).

Let them know you want to remain in their world. Do what my parents do and travel nine hours for a two-hour play and then drive nine hours back the next day. If you want to share in the lives of your adult children, do what it takes to join them in their world. Use your hard-earned money and get the kids together. Make the plans and foot the bill if you can, and use the "I won't live forever" card if you have to.

Give them this book and encourage them to read it. Tell them what you've learned and what you wished you'd known before and what you hope they'll be able to teach you.

Oh, and pray for them—without ceasing.

QUESTIONS TO CONSIDER

1. When did you realize you were no longer the director in your child's life?
2. When was the last time you told your adult child you were proud of him/her?
3. What are you willing to do to keep your family ties strong?

PART 6

Common Issues Families Are Facing and What You Can Do About Them

Without going into too much detail, let's just say that I'm in the trenches with you in battling for my family. Spiritually speaking, there are guns popping all around, missiles screaming, and the groans of casualties filling the air. What did I expect? Yesterday my son, TJ, said, "Mom, can this be the final book you have to write on spiritual warfare? Why not join the prosperity gospel movement and let's have some good times around here!"

I just might be tempted to join that bandwagon, but not quite yet. I have a few things to expose, and while some people might preach a gospel that shortcuts the value of eternity, I will not—not today (not ever). With that said, let me remind you that the following brief chapters include issues that are most common to families today. These chapters are not arranged in any particular order. Following the description of the issue, I will give you action steps, things that you can do *right now* to start winning the battle against the devil. Then I will give you Scripture promises that are applicable to that particular issue, and finally a prayer that you can make your own. If you don't see the issue you are facing, go online for more at www.LeighannMcCoy.com/Spiritual WarfareTools. Look for "Common Issues Families Are Facing and What You Can Do About Them." Other issues listed online include Unequally Yoked (One Spouse Is Not a Christ Follower), Cutting and Other Anxiety Disorders, Negative Media Influences, Materialism, Sibling Rivalry, Bullying, Dating, Same-Sex Attraction, Suicide, and Pornography.

If you are dealing with one or more of these issues now, then get to work! God has given you access to divine power that destroys the Enemy. If you've jumped ahead to get right to these chapters, you will need to read this book in its entirety to understand how to appropriate the power God's given you in your life, in your family's life, and on your battlefield. But go ahead and start fighting. Do the action steps, memorize the Scripture, and pray God's Word to Him. Let the suggested prayers I've written help you present your petitions to the Lord. Pray them as they are or use them as models to create your own.

May God be glorified in your home!

Busyness

When I took my own little survey on my author Facebook page, I discovered that the number one issue facing families today is busyness. It isn't unusual for our families to be going in three or four different directions every day of the week. Fast-food restaurants take full advantage of our busyness by offering five burgers for five bucks on Tuesdays, half-price hot dogs on Thursdays, and balloon animals for kids on Fridays. They know that we are too busy to cook and eat our meals at the dinner table together.

We seem to have decided that activities outside the home are healthy, but do we know that activities in the home are healthy too? If your family suffers from too much time with others and too little time with each other, be brave and make a change. You can't rear your children in the fear and admonition of the Lord if you aren't spending lots of time together.

Tips for Winning the Battle of the Bulge in Your Family's Schedule

- **Make your decisions together.** If you want more time at home, you will have to say no to some of the activities you've most likely enjoyed. Discuss your choices together and let your children have some input.

- **Make your adjustments gradually.** Once you've determined what to stop doing, make the changes in between seasons. Go ahead and finish the dance recital, then take some time off of ballet or tap. Play the softball tournament, then take a season of rest.

- **Put priority on a sense of belonging.** Be careful not to cater to the remarkable talent of one child to the neglect of another. If you elevate one child beyond the others and put the family in orbit around that child's life, you risk alienating that child from the others. You may give her the world where softball is concerned, but she will miss the value of sacrificing for the others. We develop a deep sense of belonging when we have to learn the give-and-take of living our lives together. I know one family that let each child play a sport each season, but two children couldn't play at the same time. During that child's sport, the others supported him. Later, when it was one of his sibling's turns, he supported them.

- **Establish simple family routines.** When I was a little girl, my mother cooked breakfast and we ate together as a family. We have friends who have seven children. On Friday nights their family celebrates the Shabbat by eating dinner together and participating in a family discussion. Friends can be invited to join the family for their Shabbat, but family members cannot be absent. The teenage children accepted this incredible family commitment because it was established when they were preschoolers.

Verses to Add to Your Arsenal When You Fight the Battle of Busyness

Teach us to number our days, that we may gain a heart of wisdom.

Psalm 90:12

Be still, and know that I am God; I will be exalted among the nations, I will be exalted in the earth.

Psalm 46:10

The plans of the diligent lead to profit as surely as haste leads to poverty.

Proverbs 21:5

There is a time for everything, and a season for every activity under the heavens.

Ecclesiastes 3:1

Let us not become weary in doing good, for at the proper time we will reap a harvest if we do not give up.

Galatians 6:9

PRAYER

Father, forgive us for being so busy we forget that you are God. Thank you for this family. Thank you for putting us together with one another and for allowing us to spend this season of life with all of us under one roof. I know that the day will come when we no longer live in one place. Teach us to number our days so that we make the most of them. O God, give us wisdom to know when to say yes and when to say no. And let us carefully weigh the noes that come with the yeses and the yeses that come with the noes. Give us patience as we adjust our schedules, and reward the time that we spend with one another. Let us take seriously your command that we teach our children your ways while they are living with us. We love you, Lord, and want to honor you with our family's time. In Jesus' powerful name we pray. Amen.

Loneliness

One of the hardest feelings to overcome is the feeling of loneliness, especially when you, your spouse, or one of your children are experiencing loneliness in the home. The family is supposed to be the one place where you can be yourself, be accepted, feel safe, and share life together. But that is not always the case. The devil loves loneliness. For when he isolates one person from the protection of the herd, he can gain an advantage over them.

It is all too easy for families that are too busy to miss the fact that one or more of their family members might suffer loneliness. Look around your home. Are there times when someone separates himself from the others? Maybe the family is watching television together and one child goes to his room. That isn't a concern unless it's the same child every time. Husbands, if your wife is not talking to you, she might be lonely. Women need to talk. I've heard that we use 20,000 words a day compared to only 7,000 by men. The world would be a quiet place if women curbed their talking! I am only saying that to let you know that silence is not golden if it exists between you and your wife.

The great truth is that loneliness can be overcome.

Things You Can Do to Overcome Loneliness in Your Home

- **Be a student of your children.** Discover their love languages,[1] share in their interests, and expect siblings to do the same.
- **Nurture an all-for-one-and-one-for-all family mindset.** Be intentional in sacrificing for one another. Set the example for your children by going above and beyond to serve your spouse when he or she is sick, overwhelmed, or in need of extra patience. Expect this from your children, and reward them when they do this with one another. My husband was in a serious car accident the day we arrived at my sister's house to enjoy "cousins camp." My children had been looking forward to our time together for weeks. When I discovered the extent of Tom's injuries, I drove us home. I explained to my disappointed children that we were all in this together, and that when Dad needed us, we needed to be there for him.
- **Create memories together.** When our family took a trip to Arizona, we had all kinds of adventures. I took the time to scrapbook our pictures, and although we've taken many trips since then, to this day we still flip the pages of that book and remember the fun we had on that trip together.
- **Have a whatever-it-takes mentality.** Do whatever you need to do to help the lonely overcome her loneliness. Go out of your way to spend time together, to listen, to encourage, and to cheer. Your whatever-it-takes mentality might be as simple as baking her favorite cake or as complicated as learning to love Civil War history.

Verses to Add to Your Arsenal When You Are Overcoming Loneliness

Be strong and courageous. Do not be afraid or terrified because of them, for the Lord your God goes with you; he will never leave you nor forsake you.

Deuteronomy 31:6

For the sake of his great name the Lord will not reject his people, because the Lord was pleased to make you his own.

1 Samuel 12:22

Turn to me and be gracious to me, for I am lonely and afflicted.

Psalm 25:16

Who shall separate us from the love of Christ? Shall trouble or hardship or persecution or famine or nakedness or danger or sword? As it is written, "For your sake we face death all day long; we are considered as sheep to be slaughtered." No, in all these things we are more than conquerors through him who loved us. For I am convinced that neither death nor life, neither angels nor demons, neither the present nor the future, nor any powers, neither height nor depth, nor anything else in all creation, will be able to separate us from the love of God that is in Christ Jesus our Lord.

Romans 8:35–39

So do not fear, for I am with you; do not be dismayed, for I am your God. I will strengthen you and help you; I will uphold you with my righteous right hand.

Isaiah 41:10

PRAYER

Lord, your Word says that you will never leave me or forsake me. You are a God who is near, not far away. I know you are with me. My (daughter, son, spouse) needs to know you are near. Please make yourself known to (name). Let them know that when they need to experience your love with real arms for hugs and real words for encouragement, we are here to deliver those hugs and words. Remove the barriers that keep us from being a family that shares strength and encouragement. Help us to allow the confidence we have in your Word to change the way we feel. In Jesus' name I pray. Amen.

Single Parenting

Millions of children are being reared in single-parent homes. The absence of one parent makes the family vulnerable to many of the issues I'm addressing in these chapters and scores of other issues that aren't listed. But many single parents have defeated the odds that are against them and provided their children with homes that are healthy. Children from single-parent homes can still have great families.

Things You Can Do to Succeed in Your Single-Parent Home

- **Trust God to provide you with an extra measure of blessing.** Learn to count on this supernatural provision. God has a way of providing for us when we are most aware of our desperate need for Him. Be desperately dependent and expect God to provide.

- **Receive help from outside sources.** Don't be too proud to receive help from the church, from extended family, and from friends. Even two-parent families need help at times. You rob others of blessing when you refuse their help.

- **Accept your limitations.** God doesn't expect you to be superman or superwoman just because you are a single parent. Let good (God-directed) priorities guide you. If you have to choose between listening to your child with undivided attention or making the beds, listen, and let the beds go unmade.

- **Refuse to obsess over things out of your control.** You cannot control the disappointment your children might experience from their other parent. Nor can you create your home to be like the homes that have two parents. You can, however, model for and teach your children how to manage disappointment in biblical ways. You can also celebrate the uniqueness of your own family.

Verses to Add to Your Arsenal for Single Parents

But those who trust in the Lord for help will find their strength renewed. They will rise on wings like eagles; they will run and not get weary; they will walk and not grow weak.

Isaiah 40:31 GNT

Trust in the Lord with all your heart and lean not on your own understanding; in all your ways submit to him, and he will make your paths straight.

Proverbs 3:5–6

And my God will meet all your needs according to the riches of his glory in Christ Jesus.

Philippians 4:19

The mountains and hills may crumble, but my love for you will never end; I will keep forever my promise of peace. So says the Lord who loves you.

Isaiah 54:10 GNT

For the Lord your God moves about in your camp to protect you and to deliver your enemies to you. Your camp must be holy, so that he will not see among you anything indecent and turn away from you.

Deuteronomy 23:14

PRAYER

Father, you are our heavenly Father and we need you in our earthly home. Since we are a family without a (mother/father) living here, we ask that you fill the void left by that partner's absence. We trust you to be our nurturer, our provider, our strength, and our guide. Teach me how to prove your reality to my children. Let us be confident when we appeal to you and realize that we are not handicapped by the lack of a two-parent home, but instead we are more aware of the fact that we can do absolutely nothing without you. We trust you, Lord, to be mighty in this place. Thank you for trusting us with the privilege of being family with one another. In Jesus' powerful name we pray. Amen.

29

Blended Families

When two families come together to create one, there are many challenges. However, God does some of His most redemptive work in the homes of blended families. I found a great article that describes every scenario that might create the blended family. You might enjoy reading it. You can find this article online at www.focusonthefamily.com; search "blended families."[1]

Steps You Can Take to Win the Battles in Your Blended Home

- **Be patient with your children.** Let them catch up with your enthusiasm for this new family. They have had to adjust to many changes in their lives and will need ample time to adjust to this one.
- **Set firm boundaries and stick to them.** I heard long ago that boundaries for children are like guardrails on mountain roads. I've never hit a guardrail while driving through the mountains, and if I ever did, it probably wouldn't stop

me from going over the edge. But I am so thankful they are there. Just knowing where they are gives me a sense of safety on the road. All children need firm boundaries, but children in a blended family need them more than ever. Some of their guardrails have no doubt failed them; it's your privilege to rebuild a safe and secure home where trust can grow.

- **Be prepared to love those you don't even like.** This isn't an action step only for blended families or stepparents. All parents experience moments when they seriously don't *like* their children. But in developing the unique relationship of stepparent, you are going to have to exercise God's hard-work kind of love in regard to that child who has plopped into your world with a chip on his shoulder. Read 1 Corinthians 13 and practice that kind of love.

- **Listen to hearts more than mouths.** You will need to spend much time together in order to get to know one another enough to hear each other's hearts. Take notice of the action steps under *Loneliness* and *Busyness*. Ask God to give you discernment so that you can know the *why* behind the *what* that is being said when conflict threatens to get out of control.

Scripture to Add to Your Arsenal for Blending Your Family

Likewise, husbands, live with your wives in an understanding way, showing honor to the woman as the weaker vessel, since they are heirs with you of the grace of life, so that your prayers may not be hindered.

1 Peter 3:7 ESV

Husbands, love your wives, even as Christ also loved the church, and gave himself for it; that he might sanctify and cleanse it with the washing of water by the word, that he might present it to himself a glorious church, not having spot, or wrinkle, or any such thing; but that it should be holy and without blemish. So ought men to love their wives as their own bodies. He that loveth his wife loveth himself.

Ephesians 5:25–28 KJV

Fathers, do not exasperate your children; instead, bring them up in the training and instruction of the Lord.

Ephesians 6:4

Wives, submit yourselves unto your own husbands, as unto the Lord. For the husband is the head of the wife, even as Christ is the head of the church: and he is the savior of the body.

Ephesians 5:22–23 KJV

Children, obey your parents in the Lord, for this is right. "Honor your father and mother"—which is the first commandment with a promise—so that it may go well with you and that you may enjoy long life on the earth.

Ephesians 6:1–3

PRAYER

Father, we want to be a family that honors you. Our home is already a testimony of redemption. Please make us an example to others, proving what you can do when parents trust you. Bring peace and joy into our home. Teach us to guide our children toward patience, long-suffering, and genuine compassion for one another. Give us wisdom in negotiating truces and establishing healthy boundaries. Increase our love for one another as you increase our devotion to you. We are asking that you be glorified in this house, and that we grow through our trials together. Draw each family member into a closer relationship with you. In Jesus' name we pray. Amen.

Premarital Sex

If you are aware that your child is sexually active, don't put your head in the sand and wish this situation would go away. Stand tall, gird yourself for battle, and go to war!

Action Steps You Can Take to Battle Effectively Against This Spiritual Attack

- **Lovingly confront your son or daughter.** Ask open-ended questions like, "Tell me about your relationship with _____." If your child doesn't admit his behavior (which is most likely), share your knowledge about it with him. Then, share your concerns by explaining the increased risks both physically and emotionally when people engage in sex outside of marriage. There are many resources for this online. Focus on the Family is one of the best.

- **Have a candid conversation with your child's partner and parents.** Know that this is going to be awkward and uncomfortable. But press on! Hopefully the other parents will share your concerns. If so, together discuss your concerns about your children's futures and encourage both of them to stop this behavior immediately and make wise choices.

- **Evaluate and reduce the freedom your child has found in his/her dating world.** It would be naïve to think that you can control what is happening when they are out of your sight, but you are responsible for adjusting the boundaries to make it harder for them to continue having a sexual relationship.
- **Be realistic while you are being faith-filled.** Pray and expect God to do what you cannot, but do take your child to a physician to be examined and to learn the medical risks of sex outside of marriage.

Scripture Verses to Add to Your Arsenal If Your Child Is Sexually Active

Now the works of the flesh are evident: sexual immorality, impurity, sensuality.

Galatians 5:19 ESV

For this is the will of God, your sanctification: that you abstain from sexual immorality.

1 Thessalonians 4:3 ESV

Let marriage be held in honor among all, and let the marriage bed be undefiled, for God will judge the sexually immoral and adulterous.

Hebrews 13:4 ESV

If we confess our sins, he is faithful and just to forgive us our sins and purify us from all unrighteousness.

1 John 1:9

Flee from sexual immorality. All other sins a person commits are outside the body, but whoever sins sexually, sins against their own body.

1 Corinthians 6:18

PRAYER

O God, our hearts are breaking over the reality of our child's sexual immorality. First we want to ask that you forgive (name) for blatantly disobeying your Word. We understand that their sin is detestable in your sight, for you are holy. Let us stand in the gap interceding on their behalf as we ask you to convict him/her of their sin and lead him/her to repentance. Thank you for bringing what was hidden in the darkness to the light. Give us wisdom, insight, and discernment to address this directly and firmly in such a way that our son/daughter knows beyond a shadow of a doubt that they are loved. Give our child the strength and wisdom to repent and walk away. Break any soul tie that has come as a result of this sin against their body. In Jesus' name we pray. Amen.

Divorce

God hates divorce because divorce hates you. I've walked with many women through the crisis of divorce and none of them have enjoyed the journey. While the dissolution of your marriage might feel like spiritual defeat, nothing can come against you that God can't redeem. If you will let Him, God will reveal himself to you in unimaginable ways as you suffer through this journey.

Know that better days are ahead.

Things You Can Do to Win the Battles That Arise Out of Divorce

- **Know that you are not abandoned.** The devil loves to shame you with divorce. God is for you especially now. He will walk with you, His love will cover you, and He will comfort you. Continue in your quiet time, in daily Bible reading and prayer.

- **Get support from other believers who've walked this path before you.** We were not designed to manage the hard times by ourselves. God created you to be interdependent on others. Find a group of friends who can relate to what you are feeling. Learn from them so that you can avoid the potholes scattered across this trail.

- **Assure your children that you are always a family.** Even though your family is not all living in the same house together, let your children know they still have a mother and a father and that you are still a family. Invite them to share their thoughts and feelings so that you can correct any wrong thought patterns and dispel any fears. Make sure your children understand that the divorce is not their fault. Let them know that what you all are going through is a season that will change. Let your children know what you are doing to move your family forward.

- **Let people help you with your kids.** I haven't experienced divorce, but when I was fighting cancer and my daughter was breaking our hearts, my two teenage children felt neglected and alone. Had it not been for other families inviting my children into their homes and letting them borrow their stable home environment for a season, I am not sure what we would have done. Let God meet your needs through other families who love you and your children.

Scripture Verses to Add to Your Arsenal As You Overcome the Enemy's Attacks in This Divorce

But if the unbeliever leaves, let it be so. The brother or sister is not bound in such circumstances; God has called us to live in peace. How do you know, wife, whether you will save your husband? Or, how do you know, husband, whether you will save your wife? Nevertheless, each person should live as a believer in whatever situation the Lord has assigned to them, just as God has called them.

1 Corinthians 7:15–17

For if you forgive other people when they sin against you, your heavenly Father will also forgive you. But if you do not forgive others their sins, your Father will not forgive your sins.

Matthew 6:14–15

He gives strength to the weary and increases the power of the weak.

Isaiah 40:29

My soul is weary with sorrow; strengthen me according to your word.

Psalm 119:28

But he said to me, "My grace is sufficient for you, for my power is made perfect in weakness." Therefore I will boast all the more gladly about my weaknesses, so that Christ's power may rest on me. That is why, for Christ's sake, I delight in weaknesses, in insults, in hardships, in persecutions, in difficulties. For when I am weak, then I am strong.

2 Corinthians 12:9–10

PRAYER

Father, I am broken, crushed, and feeling very much alone. But I choose to trust you to meet me where I am and to lead me on to greater things. Please heal my pain, and give me the compassion to forgive those who have caused my pain. Lord, help me to start over with a clean slate—forgetting what lies behind and pressing on. Give me friends I can trust, who will be voices to your heart and mind. Show me those people, and show me to them. Help me to hear your voice as I take this journey. I choose to trust you to meet every need we have—financial, emotional, and spiritual. Help me to have enough strength to be attentive to my children's hearts as well. Thank you for the promise that we will not remain in this place forever. In Jesus' name I pray. Amen.

Lack of Communication

Oh, how the devil loves to meddle with our ability to communicate with one another. Jesus called him the Father of Lies. The issue of communication might be at the root of many other issues. Without good communication, many other things can get out of order.

Things You Can Do to Increase Healthy Communication in Your Home

- **Eat dinner together.** Preferably this would be a sit-down-at-the-table meal together on a routine basis. Don't use this time to discuss anything difficult, just have fun sharing with one another.
- **Get rid of distractions.** When you want to communicate with one another, put away the electronics. Declare an electronic-free zone. I've started doing this in my Sunday school class of seventh grade girls, and it's truly incredible how much more they interact with each other when they put away their phones.
- **Have some intentional family discussions.** One of the easiest topics of discussion is to share highs and lows from your day

(or week). With older children you might try this one: Take turns telling one another something you might start, something you might stop, and something you might continue. We did this on a family vacation, and had fun while learning a lot about ourselves.

- **LISTEN!** Your children will talk as long as they think they are being heard. There is nothing more frustrating than a parent who says he wants to gain a better understanding of his child only to get into a conversation and do all the talking. If this is you, your son or daughter has most likely endured the frustration of longing to be heard and is beginning to shut you out.

Scripture Verses to Add to Your Arsenal As You Overcome the Attack on Your Family's Communication

Instead, speaking the truth in love, we will grow to become in every respect the mature body of him who is the head, that is, Christ.

Ephesians 4:15

Better is open rebuke than hidden love. Wounds from a friend can be trusted, but an enemy multiplies kisses.

Proverbs 27:5–6

Do to others as you would have them do to you.

Luke 6:31

Be completely humble and gentle; be patient, bearing with one another in love.

Ephesians 4:2

For the Spirit God gave us does not make us timid, but gives us power, love and self-discipline.

2 Timothy 1:7

PRAYER

Father, you know that we have a difficult time communicating. You also know that we get our feelings hurt, that we often say things we don't mean, and that many times we wish we could take back things that we've said. Please forgive us where we mess up. Help us to communicate more clearly with one another. Let us speak the truth in love. And when the truth is painful, give us compassion. When someone's words hurt us, let us be quick to forgive. Grow our trust with one another so that we can keep the Enemy from creating a web of deception between us. O God, please let all lies and deception be swallowed up in truth. In Jesus' powerful name I pray. Amen.

Substance Abuse
and Addictions

I cannot tell you how many times I've received messages from distressed parents whose children have fallen victim to the Enemy's attacks in the area of substance abuse and addiction. One mother I know has worn herself out praying over her son. Many days she does not know if he is alive or dead. Recently I received a message from another mom whose son seems determined to kill himself or someone else as a result of his drug addiction.

"He has stolen money, threatened to kill himself if we punish him, wrecked his car twice, and missed more school than he attended."

If you suffer from this same attack, I know you feel her pain.

But I've also met a beautiful young woman who grew up in a very southern (Baptist) home. As a young adult, she dated a boy who was "edgy." He introduced her to marijuana and then to meth. She experienced seven tortuous years, many that she does not remember. But she told me the other night that she was able to return to church and a home Bible study because her parents prayed for her, loved her (suffered and wept over her), and gave her a strong spiritual foundation in life.

Things You Can Do to Defeat the Enemy With Regard to Substance Abuse and Addiction in Your Home

- **Recognize your limitations.** While you cannot fix your child, you can take full advantage of this trial, claiming all that the Bible promises through it. (See Romans 5:3–5.)
- **Pray.** Only God has the power to change hearts. Only God. *God has the power to change hearts!*
- **Seek professional counseling for your child.** The most successful treatment programs engage the family in the process. So look for counseling that includes the family. Look for this article on Focus on the Family's website: "Dealing With a Teen Who Struggles With Drug Addiction."[1]
- **Know your resources!** Tap into them sooner rather than later. Don't wait until your child's poor choices have ruined your home. They will not get better without help. To help find the resources that are right for you, do a web search for substance abuse rehab centers. Most people will find plenty of options near home.

Scripture to Use When Fighting the Battle Against Substance Abuse and Addiction in Your Family

Not only so, but we also glory in our sufferings, because we know that suffering produces perseverance; perseverance, character; and character, hope. And hope does not put us to shame, because God's love has been poured out into our hearts through the Holy Spirit, who has been given to us.

Romans 5:3–5

Do not be anxious about anything, but in every situation, by prayer and petition, with thanksgiving, present your requests to God. And the peace of God, which transcends all understanding, will guard your hearts and your minds in Christ Jesus.

Philippians 4:6–7

If you need wisdom, ask our generous God, and he will give it to you. He will not rebuke you for asking.

James 1:5 NLT

I have set the Lord always before me; because he is at my right hand, I shall not be shaken.

Psalm 16:8 ESV

You will keep in perfect peace those whose minds are steadfast, because they trust in you.

Isaiah 26:3

PRAYER

O God, please come near to me now. Like the mother who followed hard after you and your disciples, then begged, "It's my daughter!" I'm following hard after you and pleading, "It's my son/daughter!" Save him/her. Give me the courage to seek professional help. Give my spouse and me one mind and one heart concerning our child. Guard my mind from rushing forward to a future known only to you. And empower me to take the thoughts of the past captive to the lordship of Christ. I choose to trust that you have already forgiven any shortcomings in me. I refuse to believe that our current circumstances are payback or punishment or anything else the devil tempts me to label them. I trust that you will sustain us during these days and bring us out on the other side, proven and strong. In Jesus' name I pray. Amen.

Crisis Pregnancy
and Abortion

I wish I didn't have personal experience with this issue, but I do. I have an immediate family member who told me about her abortion seventeen years after she'd had it. I had no idea. I grieved over the baby who never was and over the breach I never knew existed between this family member and me. It hurt me to realize she was going through such a difficult season in her life and she didn't feel close enough to me to let me share that season with her.

Then, my own daughter discovered she was pregnant a month after she graduated from high school. She became a mother at eighteen. Those were difficult days, not because she was pregnant, but because the devil did all he could do to keep us disconnected from each other.

The primary issue you face if you're dealing with a crisis pregnancy or an abortion is the brokenness you experience in your relationship with one another. The problem is not the baby. Of course, dreams have been shattered and life has gotten complicated. But the devil delights in your crisis by taking full advantage of the sexual sin that resulted in the pregnancy and pitching you forward into a reckless imaginary journey to the unknown future. He plans a great big party and brings shame, regret, guilt, disappointment, and anger to the dance. You may have to attend the party; you might not have a choice. But don't dance with the devil or any of his cohorts if you find yourself dealing with this issue.

Things You Can Do to Defeat the Enemy If You Are Dealing With a Crisis Pregnancy or an Abortion

- **Realize that you are on a journey.** The moment you discover your son or daughter has brought this issue home is just one landmark on a long hike. This is not an event; it's a series of daily decisions that direct your relationship and your lives.
- **Keep your primary objective front and center in your mind.** Your primary objective is to grow in your relationship with your son/daughter and for your son/daughter to grow in his/her relationship with the Lord.
- **Understand and help your son/daughter understand that being pregnant out of wedlock is not a sin.** Having sex outside of marriage is a sin, but the pregnancy that resulted from that sin is not. The baby who comes from that pregnancy was created in the heart of God. This is grace.
- **God is bigger than all of this.** No matter if your child is pregnant or if she has had an abortion, God is still God and He's got a plan for all of this. It's going to be hard, but it's going to be good if you choose to go the distance with Him.

Scripture to Use When Fighting the Battle of Crisis Pregnancy and Abortion

I can do all this through him who gives me strength.

Philippians 4:13

God is our refuge and strength, an ever-present help in trouble.

Psalm 46:1

For you created my inmost being; you knit me together in my mother's womb. I praise you because I am fearfully and wonderfully made; your works are wonderful, I know that full well. My frame was not hidden from you when I was made in the secret place, when I was woven together in the depths of the earth. Your eyes saw my unformed body; all the days ordained for me were written in your book before one of them came to be. How precious to me are your thoughts, God! How vast is the sum of them! Were I to count them, they would outnumber the grains of sand—when I awake, I am still with you.

Psalm 139:13–18

Plans fail for lack of counsel, but with many advisers they succeed.

Proverbs 15:22

"For my thoughts are not your thoughts, neither are your ways my ways," declares the Lord. "As the heavens are higher than the earth, so are my ways higher than your ways and my thoughts than your thoughts."

Isaiah 55:8–9

PRAYER

O God, my heart is broken. I am so disappointed. All the dreams I had for my son/daughter are fading away. Please come close and lend me your compassion and your mercy. Cover me with your wisdom and your love. Examine my heart, and remove all condemnation, shame, pride, and blame. Fill me afresh with your Spirit. Give me your heart and your mind in this situation. Help me to reflect your love to my son/daughter. Use this unexpected event to draw me and my son/daughter, and everyone else in our family, closer to one another and to you. Restore the brokenness and let us be better than we could have ever been before this happened. In Jesus' name I pray. Amen.

35

Cancer, Death,
and Chronic Illness

Unfortunately I have personal experience with this issue too. I was diagnosed with cancer in 2010 and again in 2012. My sister was diagnosed in 2013 and died in 2015. My mother has suffered with arthritis since she was in her early forties. When I was diagnosed with colon cancer, my greatest dread was having to tell my children. I knew that the cancer I had to fight was going to change their lives forever.

One of the assistants from Dr. Caudill's office (the gastroenterologist who diagnosed the cancer) was a family friend. Many years ago my husband, Tom, led her husband to the Lord at their kitchen table. The night we were going to tell our children about my diagnosis, Sharon brought our family dinner from Cracker Barrel, yummy southern comfort food. When we told all three of our children that we needed them home for dinner, they knew something was amiss. After we enjoyed our dinner, Tom explained to them that the doctor had found cancer in my colon. At the time, we didn't know the extent of the disease, and we didn't know my prognosis. All we knew was that I was seriously sick and that this was the beginning of a new reality for our family. I'll never forget that night.

Cancer, death, and chronic illness are difficult issues that every family will eventually face to one degree or another. These trials are part of life. But if you are not prepared, they can be used by Satan to gain footholds in your children's lives. Don't let him do that.

Things You Can Do to Defeat the Enemy When He Attacks Your Family Through Cancer, Death, or Chronic Illness

- **Remember that God is still God.** I'll never forget the people I met in the chemo lab. One man had cancer in his liver, and was dealing with the reality that he might not live two years. He told me about having his daughters adjust their plans for the big family reunion. He urged them to have it sooner because of his limited time left. He smiled and said, "No matter what happens to me, cancer is still spelled with a little *c* and God is still spelled with a big G!" Cancer, death, and chronic disease do not diminish the perfect power of God.

  Just because you or someone in your family has cancer does not mean that your faith has failed or that God has forgotten you. God has invited you to know and serve Him like never before. Consider this quote:

  > We can open our eyes and hearts. God relishes surprise. We want lives of simple, predictable ease—smooth, even trails as far as the eye can see—but God likes to go off-road. He provokes us with twists and turns. He places us in predicaments that seem to defy our endurance and comprehension—and yet don't. By his love and grace, we persevere. The challenges that make our hearts leap and stomachs churn invariably

strengthen our faith and grant measures of wisdom and joy we would not experience otherwise.[1]

This is a quote from Tony Snow, press secretary for the Bush administration. Snow died of colon cancer at the age of fifty-three.

- **Live in the moment.** One of the gifts that cancer delivers is the realization that we are mortal creatures and that our lives here on earth are temporary. Death delivers the same message. When my nephew died in a car accident that also killed two of his friends, the young people wailed at his funeral. They were surprised and devastated by the reality of life's uncertainties. Because life is fragile, and everyone is "terminally ill," learn to live in the moment. Stop watching the time, stop worrying so much over things that are out of your control or suspended in the vapor of an imaginary tomorrow. Enjoy the simple things in life like laughter, time together with family and friends, and cupcakes.

- **Cherish relationships more than anything.** When my sister was dying, my family just wanted to be together. Suddenly all the little things that drove us crazy about each other didn't matter so much anymore. We learned to see one another with our hearts rather than our heads. We discovered that our differences were what made us interesting rather than wrong.

  When I was fighting cancer, one of my favorite people was my granddaughter Misty. She was a toddler, and she didn't know what was going on. But she could sit for hours with me on the couch and play quietly. Just being together was enough for both of us. Appreciate time together, and express the love you have for one another.

- **Embrace the reality of eternity.** Don't miss this incredible opportunity to be a witness to the world. You don't face certain death, but rather a transition from this world to the next. You've been born again, and therefore you will live.

Your body will die, but you get to live forever. When my sister was nearing her final days on earth, my mother said, "If I am trusting God at all, I have to trust Him with it all." She prayed to have the strength to trust Him no matter the outcome of my sister's disease.

When I sat at dinner and shared the news of my cancer diagnosis with my children, I said, "I've lived more in my forty-six years than most people live in a hundred. If God takes me out, I will not be cheated. I've lived a great life, and God has been good to me. The absolute worst thing you could ever do would be to get angry with God because of me. Honor me by choosing God and living your lives for Him." We face death differently because we know there is life just on the other side.

Scripture to Use When Fighting Cancer, Death, or Chronic Illness

When I was going through chemo treatment, my mind grew foggy and I couldn't think like I normally do. I still taught the Wednesday night women's study at my church on the weeks opposite of treatment. And to keep my mind sharp, I challenged myself to memorize Psalm 62. There are twelve verses and there were twelve treatments. I figured I could memorize a verse for each treatment. I quoted that Psalm every Wednesday night that I sat before the group to teach. It is a great Psalm to memorize, especially if cancer or other serious illness strikes your home.

> Truly my soul finds rest in God; my salvation comes from him. Truly he is my rock and my salvation; he is my fortress, I will never be shaken.
>
> Psalm 62:1–2

> Being confident of this, that he who began a good work in you will carry it on to completion until the day of Christ Jesus.
>
> Philippians 1:6

Humble yourselves, therefore, under God's mighty hand, that he may lift you up in due time. Cast all your anxiety on him because he cares for you.

1 Peter 5:6–7

The Spirit himself testifies with our spirit that we are God's children. Now if we are children, then we are heirs—heirs of God and co-heirs with Christ, if indeed we share in his sufferings in order that we may also share in his glory.

Romans 8:16–17

But those who hope in the Lord will renew their strength. They will soar on wings like eagles; they will run and not grow weary, they will walk and not be faint.

Isaiah 40:31

PRAYER

O Lord, my God, thank you for being near to us now. We need you more than ever. Lead us through this journey and bring us out on the other side more intimately related to you and to one another. Give our family sweet times together. Teach us to live in the moment and to express our love to each other. Show us how to gain every eternal virtue you have for us to gain through this difficult experience. Strengthen us so that we can encourage one another, and let our faith in you sustain us. Shine your light through our lives, as others will be watching. In Jesus' name I pray. Amen.

The Prodigal Child

We enter into relationships with our children while they are helpless and completely dependent on us to meet their every need. Gradually they grow and we learn to shift our parental gears. We become directors of their lives. We choose what sports they might enjoy. We determine where they'll go to school. We choose their friends and their clothes, we insist on certain behaviors—rewarding the good ones and punishing the bad ones.

And when they continue to grow, we gradually let go of more and more of those areas and we become advisers in their lives. We encourage them to make wise choices and we celebrate when they do. We expand their borders and give them more freedom. We let them know that we expect them to continue behaving in certain ways, and we might still take away privileges and freedoms when they behave in ways that are contrary to what we think is best for them.

But when our children break away from the natural progression toward adulthood, we are toppled from our advisory roles. They may choose to disregard our advice and go their own way. So we are not only left with the agony of knowing the heartache and pain their foolishness will produce but also with being "fired" from our God-given parental role.

We find ourselves without a job! We are ousted! Rejected—given the pink slip.

If you've been fired by your own child, take heart, you're in good company. God was fired many times, and He was the perfect parent. Don't let Satan defeat you just because you got to experience the heart of God in a personal way.

Things You Can Do to Defeat Satan's Attack When You Have a Prodigal Child

- **Know the difference between loving and enabling.** While your child is choosing to live in his prodigal season, he may be angry, manipulative, selfish, rude, and demanding. To tolerate this behavior is *not* love. Love sets healthy boundaries and stands firm when those boundaries are breached. Ask God to give you discernment to know when to set boundaries and how to enforce them.

- **Don't blame yourself.** It is very natural to replay the last fifteen, eighteen, or twenty years of your child's life and reinterpret every parenting mistake. Don't do this! You cannot take responsibility that is not yours. To blame yourself is to give yourself undue power. You most likely did the best you knew to do at the time, every day of your child's life. He or she is making their *own* decisions in spite of your good parenting. Choose to take those memories captive to the lordship of Christ and replace the walk down memory lane with concerted effort to memorize Scripture that you can pray over.

- **Follow the biblical example.** Jesus told a powerful parable about a prodigal son who left his father's home with his share of his family inheritance, then squandered his father's riches on wild living. It wasn't until this young man found himself in a pig pen that he decided to return home. While he was away he never lost sleep over his father. While he was away he never felt remorse over his sin. In fact, his hunger sent him home, not his conscience.

His father gave him his wealth, watched his son leave, and then waited anxiously for his return. The prodigal's father longed for his son's return. Having been in this man's sandals, I can imagine what he did. (He watched Facebook and Instagram for signs of his son's well-being!) He prayed that *this day* would be the day of his return and kept his eyes on the road. He didn't go after him and he didn't send spies to check on him. The father let his son go.

A prodigal's parents must let their child go. You really don't have a choice. Going after him will only prolong the time it takes for him to get to his God-ordained pig pen. You can't bring him back. Although the brokenness in your relationship is of utmost importance, the brokenness in his relationship with God is more important. Leave room for God to work. As hard as this might be, turn your eyes (your head and your heart) to other worthwhile endeavors while you pray for your prodigal's repentance and return.

- **Build a united front with your spouse.** The devil's already got a hold on your child—he's after *you* now. Don't let him mess with your marriage. You may be tempted to spend the bulk of your time talking about the ache that you share over your prodigal, but this will eventually drain you. Determine to do some things together without allowing conversation about your child's behavior to monopolize your activities. Determine to be in agreement on how you will relate to your prodigal and what you will and will not give him/her.

Scripture You Can Use in Dealing With Your Prodigal Child

Wait for the Lord; be strong and take heart and wait for the Lord.

Psalm 27:14

Cast your cares on the Lord and he will sustain you; he will never let the righteous be shaken.

Psalm 55:22

Trust in the Lord with all your heart and lean not on your own understanding; in all your ways submit to him, and he will make your paths straight.

Proverbs 3:5–6

Do not be afraid, for I am with you; I will bring your children from the east and gather you from the west. I will say to the north, "Give them up!" and to the south, "Do not hold them back." Bring my sons from afar and my daughters from the ends of the earth.

Isaiah 43:5–6

Because of the Lord's great love we are not consumed, for his compassions never fail. They are new every morning; great is your faithfulness. I say to myself, "The Lord is my portion; therefore I wait for him." The Lord is good to those whose hope is in him, to the one who seeks him; it is good to wait quietly for the salvation of the Lord. [I'm memorizing this one right now!]

Lamentations 3:22–26

PRAYER

O God, please! Bring my son/daughter to yourself. I feel like she's headed full speed ahead toward disaster. Watching her make such a mess of her life is painful beyond words. The things he says, the accusations he makes, the threats, the lies—they are too much for me to bear. And yet my hope is in you. You are my fortress, you are my strength, and you are my calm assurance. Empower me to steward this trial in a way that brings you glory. As I wait on your certain rescue, as I anticipate my son/daughter's return, let my heart be strengthened and my mind determined to live like I'm convinced of the certainty of your promises. Teach me to pour my love into my spouse and other children, and to demonstrate my confidence in you by genuinely giving him/her to you every minute my mind tends to wander and my heart begs to break. I trust you and I love you. Amen.

Financial Stress and Debt

We own a small ski boat. It was built in 1989, and in its day she was a beauty. Of course, we consider her beautiful still. She is reliable (most of the time) and we have many great days on the lake. If you've ever driven a boat, you know that it's different than driving a car. Boats don't have brakes for one thing, and lakes have wakes. The wake is the swell of water that's created by other boats. When boating, you have to be aware of these wakes and skilled at maneuvering over them. I've discovered that the best way to conquer a wake is to drive straight at it. If you get frightened and turn to miss it, the wake might spill over the side of your boat, soaking all your passengers. Financial stress and debt might do the same thing.

The best way to approach the problem of your family's financial crisis is head on. If you ignore it or get frightened by it, the weight of that debt is going to spill over into your relationships and soak all your "passengers." This is a battle you can win. Face it squarely and meet it head on.

Things You Can Do to Defeat the Devil and End the Financial Crisis in Your Home

- **Take captive every thought.** Don't let your imagination run wild with "what if" scenarios. The God who knows the number of hairs on your head (that changes every minute) is fully aware of your financial crisis. He alone knows what the future holds, and He is eager to meet your needs. Give your anxious thoughts to Him. Remember, God fed the Israelites manna in the wilderness that fell daily. If you have shelter and food today, God is providing for you. The same God who is providing today will be providing when tomorrow becomes today.

- **Resist the urge to medicate your stress.** Don't make your situation worse by overeating, drinking, or spending what you don't have to lessen the pain and stress of your situation. This will only lead to increased stress as you deal with the problems created by your "stress relievers." Find constructive ways to deal with your stress. Take walks, listen to music, chase fireflies, or roast marshmallows over an open fire.

- **Audit your family finances.** Take a deep breath, pray, and deal with the facts and figures. Take an assessment of your income and expenses. Put the facts on paper, and ask God to replace the feelings of anxiety and despair with faith and hope. Evaluate the facts with these questions: What can we do to consolidate our debt? Is there anything we can do to eliminate high interest? How might we increase our income? What can we do to decrease our expenses? Get the entire family in on the conversation. This is a great time for your children to see how the family works together to overcome difficulties. Even if your child's sacrifice doesn't make a dent in the financial burden, the sacrifice itself will pay rich dividends for him as he develops a generous spirit.

- **Take advantage of resources.** There are many resources online and through churches that help families take charge of their finances. Take advantage of these resources. Some I have discovered are www.crown.org; www.daveramsey.com, www.eChristianFinance.com, and www.MasterYourMoney.com.

Scripture to Take to Battle for Your Finances

For where your treasure is, there your heart will be also.

Matthew 6:21

"Bring the whole tithe into the storehouse, that there may be food in my house. Test me in this," says the Lord Almighty, "and see if I will not throw open the floodgates of heaven and pour out so much blessing that there will not be room enough to store it."

Malachi 3:10

Better the little that the righteous have than the wealth of many wicked; for the power of the wicked will be broken, but the Lord upholds the righteous.

Psalm 37:16–17

Keep your lives free from the love of money and be content with what you have, because God has said, "Never will I leave you; never will I forsake you."

Hebrews 13:5

No one can serve two masters. Either you will hate the one and serve the other, or you will be devoted to the one and despise the other. You cannot serve God and money.

Matthew 6:24

PRAYER

Father, first I want to thank you. Thank you for hearing our prayers, thank you for answering us when we call. Thank you for being a God who gives. Thank you for your generosity expressed over and over again to us. Lord, we confess our desperate need for your help. We place our hope and our trust in you. Give us clarity, give us creativity, give us wisdom and knowledge. Show us where we need to let go, and where we need to hold tight. Show us how to decrease our expenses and increase our income. Wipe away the pride that keeps us from receiving help. And, Lord, when we get on the other side of this crisis may we be generous toward others. In Jesus' name we pray. Amen.

(38)

Dealing With Extended Family . . . In-Laws

A small group at my church invited me and a friend to come and offer our wisdom. My friend and I humbly accepted their invitation as we also humbly accepted the fact that we'd passed over to the "age of wisdom." As the young wives and mothers presented their questions, I realized that I'd forgotten how difficult it is to deal with those early years of establishing your family. My husband and I have been married so long and we've so established the Mc-Coys as a family unit that I forgot what it was like to be a Keesee (my unusual maiden name) married to a McCoy.

If you think about it, family is a strange experience. You are born into one family where your parents are living the lives they've chosen to live with the person they've chosen to live it with. They are making adjustments to each other and creating a family identity for you. Then you grow up and choose a partner and create a new family. You leave the old one and cleave to the new one. This is good, but you still have parents that spent their lives investing in yours!

What are they to do?

What are you to do with them?

Now that I'm on the wisdom side of this family dynamic, I want to assure you that this transition is much more difficult for the older parents than it is for the younger ones. For young families, life is natural. It's normal to have children, to love them, and to build a home for them. I suppose it's also natural for those children to grow up and leave home, but we don't all prepare well for that to happen. It's a transition for everyone. And with all transitions, this is an opportunity to honor God with your flexibility. It's also an opportunity for the devil to attack.

Things You Can Do to Defeat the Devil When He Attacks You Through Your In-Laws

- **Accept your in-laws as valuable members of your family.** I remember being a young bride and being extremely intimidated by my mother-in-law. It took some time, but gradually, as my relationship with my husband settled on solid ground, I began to appreciate her investment into her son (her baby), my husband. I chose to accept her input as an expression of her love, and I realized that my own family was more stable when I allowed room in my heart for her, and Tom allowed room in his heart for my mother.

- **Communicate with your spouse.** Talk to each other about what you expect in relationship to your parents' involvement in your life. Don't assume that you are on the same page. You might enjoy spending every Sunday after church at your mom's house while your spouse might dread it. Cooperate with each other in negotiating boundaries.

- **Develop your own relationship with each other's families.** Some experts say that it's best to let the spouse with the primary relationship deliver the messages related to boundaries and hurt feelings. This is a good idea in some situations. For instance, I didn't want grandparents spanking my preschoolers. I told my parents and Tom told his. It just went over better that way. However, it's not good to make your spouse talk to his family members *for* you. If you have an issue you need to address, talk to them yourself. While this might be uncomfortable, it will give you the best opportunity for building healthy relationships with your spouse's people. His tribe is your tribe to some degree, and your tribe is his. The sooner you realize this, accept it, and appreciate it, the sooner you will enjoy even the quirky relatives.

- **Remember that no matter how difficult your in-laws might be, you are not married to them.** Praise God! Right?! Seriously, your best defense when the pressure of the in-laws rises against your marriage is to remind yourselves that your home is your castle. You are the king and queen of your castle. If you are wise, you will accept both sets of parents as they are—complete with their strengths and weaknesses—and choose to value the homes they created and the lessons you learned there. Then, you will declare your friendly independence from them and build your own home together. When push comes to shove, remind yourself that if you live long enough, you will be the in-laws.

Scripture to Take to Battle If Satan Gets in Between You and Your Parents and/or Your In-Laws

A fool gives full vent to his spirit, but a wise man quietly holds it back.

Proverbs 29:11 ESV

He answered, "Have you not read that he who created them from the beginning made them male and female, and said, 'Therefore a man shall leave his father and his mother and hold fast to his wife, and the two shall become one flesh'? So they are no longer two but one flesh. What therefore God has joined together, let not man separate."

Matthew 19:4–6 ESV

Where there is strife, there is pride, but wisdom is found in those who take advice.

Proverbs 13:10

Iron sharpens iron, so one man sharpens another.

Proverbs 27:17 NASB

Do to others as you would like them to do to you.

Luke 6:31 NLT

PRAYER

Father, help us to appreciate our parents. Forgive us for any criticism or harshness that we've expressed to each other regarding them. I love my husband/wife and understand that their personality was impacted by their mother and father. For that I am grateful. Help me to love them like you love them. Help me to put aside contempt, competition, or insecurity where my relationship with them is concerned. Let me honor them in ways that honor my spouse and you. Show us where our healthy boundaries should be and help us to maintain them. Lord, make our hearts tender toward each other, and toward our families of origin, so that we don't miss a single treasure you have hidden for us in our relationships with them. In Jesus' name I pray. Amen.

Grandparenting

Well, if you are reading this chapter, congratulations! You've survived parenting and have been blessed with your reward: grandchildren! I cannot tell you how many grandmothers assured me that when I joined their ranks my world would be sweeter in an unimaginable way. I had my doubts at the time, for I didn't get ushered into this great army in the traditional way. My own inauguration came with great uncertainty and grief. But I discovered what every grandparent knows: Grandchildren are blessings no matter how they arrive!

If God has trusted you with grandchildren, you can be certain He has great confidence in your ability to pour a legacy of faith and love into a generation you may never know. For the values, the wisdom, the life you share with your grandchildren will one day be shared with their children and grandchildren, and that is how your life's work will continue.

Things You Can Do to Keep Satan From Winning the War Against Your Grandchildren

- **Understand and accept your role.** You are not the parent. Look in the mirror and say this aloud: "They are not my children. They are my grandchildren." As a grandparent, you are removed from the parenting role (unless you are legally parenting your grandchildren, which is different). It is your role to supplement good parenting with great grandparenting. Support your children by respecting their parenting styles and desires. Let them have the primary responsibility and support them in their good decisions. Now, if your children are doing a terrible job of parenting, hit your knees!

- **PRAY!** The most powerful thing you can do for your grandchildren is to take them to the Lord in prayer. While you can't parent them, you can give them to the very best Parent they will ever have. This is especially important to do if your grandchildren are in homes where you are concerned for their well-being. God can go where you cannot. Trust Him to go there and care for those children. And if your grandchildren are in a good, solid, Christ-centered home, still keep them in your prayers. You never know how the Enemy is going to work against them, and your resistance in prayer will serve them well on the battlefield.

- **Make memories together.** When you are with your grandchildren, put your effort into creating memories that don't center around spending lots of money. Have a tea party under the willow tree or chase fireflies at dusk. Make Christmas cookies and color Easter eggs. If you are a long-distance grandparent, send care packages and photo albums. Take pictures of the fun you have together and put them in a book. In this digital age, solid pictures on a page are very valuable.

- **Be intentional.** Pass on your spiritual legacy to your grandchildren. Be intentional with a plan and stick to it. If you get to have your preschool grandchildren spend the night, read Bible stories to them. Teach them some Sunday school songs and talk to them about your own faith. Spend one-on-one time with your elementary and teenage grandchildren. Listen to them tell you about their lives and share freely your wisdom and advice. The truth that you share will plant seeds of faith in their hearts. God will water these seeds and they will grow.

Scripture to Take to Battle As a Grandparent

Children's children are a crown to the aged, and parents are the pride of their children.

Proverbs 17:6

"They are the sons God has given me here," Joseph said to his father. Then Israel said, "Bring them to me so I may bless them."

Genesis 48:9

I am reminded of your sincere faith, which first lived in your grandmother Lois and in your mother Eunice and, I am persuaded, now lives in you also.

2 Timothy 1:5

Gray hair is a crown of splendor; it is attained in the way of righteousness.

Proverbs 16:31

But from everlasting to everlasting the Lord's love is with those who fear him, and his righteousness with their children's children.

Psalm 103:17

PRAYER

Lord, thank you for the blessing of grandchildren. Thank you for the privilege of living life long enough to be a grandparent. Help me to accept my role with all its possibilities and limitations. Help me to focus on what I can do rather than on what I cannot do, and to take full advantage of every opportunity to share my love for you with these children. Teach me to pray for them with warrior power and pour into them with purpose and passion. Increase my strength to meet the demands and sustain me with your love and power. In Jesus' name I pray. Amen.

A Final Word

I cannot tell you how much I have labored over this book. I was intentionally enthusiastic when I wrote the introduction. I told you what I'd want to know if I were reading this book. I hoped I could deliver on my promises. What you don't know is that I was fighting an intense battle when I wrote those words, and throughout the writing of this manuscript, the battle grew worse. I made a commitment not to talk about it specifically, and I'm going to keep that commitment. I anticipated that I would be under attack during my writing; I even mentioned my apprehension in the introduction.

What I didn't anticipate was the victory I was going to realize as I penned these pages. The further I got into the chapters, the more this book started taking a direction of its own (my books tend to do that). God spoon-fed me spiritual truths, and after I'd written the entire book, I printed it, placed the printed pages into notebooks, and reread what I'd written as I edited. It was during this rereading and editing process that God showed me the illustrations I shared with you in chapter 7. What started as crude drawings were brought to life by the graphic designers and are an expression of my "aha" moments. All the pieces of the spiritual warfare puzzle came together and I realized exactly how this all works. I saw the limits of power on earth, the limits of the power of the spirits of the air, and then the supreme position and power of God. I finally understood that when Jesus came to earth to bring us to God, He opened our way to access the power of God! For years I'd been wondering about the resurrection power the New Testament writers tell us is ours. I get it now!! We have access to the supreme power of the universe, and God invites us to exercise it.

It is my prayer that as you read this book, you got it too.

My war is still waging; in fact, it's more intense now than it has ever been. This past weekend I have prayed like never before. But my prayers have not been desperate, they have been powerful. I have applied the principles I've shared with you in this book, and I am convinced that battles have been won. I know that strongholds have been broken and victories are about to be announced on the battlefield where I've been fighting. God's about to get some glory here!

My heartbreaking situation relates to my family (of course). And as I type these words, the circumstances that surround me tell me that I am about to experience brokenness in my home like I have never experienced before. But my eyes are on the Lord. So instead of dreading the worst, I am expecting walls to crumble any minute. Isaiah 60:22 says, "I am the Lord; in its time I will do this swiftly." When I keep my eyes on Jesus I am confident, for He is my direct access to heaven's power, and the devil doesn't have a chance against God.

Right now, I'm getting ready to send the manuscript to the publisher. Two hours ago, I left my house and took a walk. I cried. I begged God to perform a miracle, for I just *knew* that He wanted me to be able to report a victory here. But God was silent, so I just asked Him to tell me something so I'd know He was there.

I got nothing.

After that I just walked. I smelled freshly cut hay mingled with cow manure and listened to birds and bugs and a lawn mower in the distance. But when I got to my front yard, God spoke to me. This is what He said: "Truly I tell you, whatever you bind on earth will be bound in heaven, and whatever you loose on earth will be loosed in heaven" (Matthew 18:18).

This verse has baffled me for years. But when God brought it to mind today, I connected the truth of God's Word with an illustration He gave me in my yard.

I noticed a few days ago that while I was out of town my morning glory had been weedwacked by the people who mowed our grass while we were gone. "Don't they know the difference between a weed and a morning glory?!" I asked Tom. I'd seen the vine still draped on the fence, but it was wilted because it had been whacked with a Weedwacker.

God reminded me of my wilted morning glory. He said that even though my situation seems to be worse tonight than it was yesterday, and no better yesterday than it was the day before or five years before, there was a battle won *this day* in the heavenlies. I fought the spiritual battle and I whacked the weed that has been choking my heart for many years. The weed may look alive tonight, but it will wilt.

"What you bind on earth will be bound in heaven."

For some time I've been tormented over what I believed was lost in this war. But we have another vine growing in our yard; it's coming out of the compost pile. I'm not a gardener, so my compost pile is never used for anything other than a place to dump dead flowers and rotten veggies. It's the burial ground for pumpkins in the fall. This summer, while we weren't looking, God grew a great big vine out of that compost pile. Tom was mowing this morning when he texted me to come and see this:

A pumpkin vine is growing out of the compost. And God said to me, "Whatever you loose on earth will be loosed in heaven." That pumpkin proves that God alone is able to grow great things out of piles of dead stuff.

Today my circumstances didn't seem to change. Lies still maintain their power; truth is still held at bay. But what's feeding those lies has been severed, and in a while they will lose their power (just like my morning glory vine will die). For many years God's fruit has seemingly been left to rot in my child's heart and mind, but out of the deadness, God brings incredible life. The seeds that were planted will bear fruit in due season, and there's nothing the devil can do to stop that from happening.

> Truly I tell you, whatever you bind on earth will be bound in heaven, and whatever you loose on earth will be loosed in heaven.
>
> Matthew 18:18

For many years I didn't know anything about spiritual warfare. And then I knew just enough to get me toe-to-toe with the darkness. I was like an untrained soldier, wide-eyed and trembling. But oh, my friend, today I am a warrior! I have fought with my faith that copes and I've discovered that my faith will cope. But from now on I am fighting with a faith that conquers and I am certain my faith will conquer.

What about you? I would imagine you've faced some giants who've been heckling your family far too long.

God is above all power and authority. He rules. And when you allow Him to rule over your life, He will exercise His authority and power through you. Stop coping and start conquering. The same God who enabled David to kill Goliath is the God who will rescue you.

> All those gathered here will know that it is not by sword or spear that the Lord saves; for the battle is the Lord's, and he will give all of you into our hands.
>
> 1 Samuel 17:47

Today is November 29, 2015. I am completing my final edit on this book and am thrilled to tell you that a few weeks ago my husband called me (I was out of town) and said, "Leighann, God has answered our prayers." He has done all that He promised He would do, and today I am living on the other side of an incredibly painful battle that involved my child and lasted for many years. God is good! He rescued us. This was the Lord's battle and He won it. I pray that He will do the same for you.

Notes

Chapter 1: You're Not Crazy; There Really Is a Battle Waging

1. Tony Evans in Jim Dailey, "The Reality of Spiritual Warfare," *Decision Magazine*, February 2005, billygraham.org/decision-magazine/february-2005/the-reality-of-spiritual-warfare.

Chapter 2: Did God Create the Devil?

1. Richard J. Foster, *Prayers From the Heart* (New York: HarperCollins, 1994), 24.

Chapter 3: When and How Was the War Won, and Why Do We Fight Today?

1. John Piper, "What Is God's Glory?" Desiring God, July 22, 2014, www.desiringgod.org/interviews/what-is-god-s-glory.
2. Robert Jeffress, *The Divine Defense* (Colorado Springs: Waterbrook, 2006), 63.
3. Elise, "To the Parents of Prodigal Children," Redeeming the Days, http://redeemingthedays.blogspot.com/2011/09/to-parents-of-prodigal-children.html.

Chapter 4: Three Reasons You're Losing Your Battles

1. Robertson McQuilkin, *Life in the Spirit* (Nashville: Broadman and Holman, 2000), 15.

Chapter 5: The Battle Really Is All in Your Head

1. Neil Anderson, *The Bondage Breaker* (Eugene, OR: Harvest House, 2000), 11, emphasis mine.
2. Maurice D'Aoustand, "Hoodwinked During America's Civil War: Confederate Military Deception," *Civil War Times*, June 2006, www.historynet.com/hoodwinked-during-americas-civil-war-confederate-military-deception.htm.
3. Andrew Wommack, "Spiritual Authority," Andrew Wommack Ministries, www.awmi.net/reading/teaching-articles/spiritual_authority.

Chapter 7: What on Earth Is Spiritual Authority?

1. "Rome Celebrates the Vanquishing of the Jews, AD 71," Eyewitness to History, www.eyewitnesstohistory.com/rometriumph.htm.

Chapter 8: How Do We Exercise Spiritual Authority?

1. Richard Foster, "Crucifying Our Will," *Knowing & Doing*, Fall 2005, www.cslewisinstitute.org/webfm_send/433.
2. Catherine Marshall, "The Prayer of Relinquishment," *Guideposts*, www.guideposts.org/faith/prayer/how-to-pray-effectively/the-prayer-of-relinquishment.
3. Ibid.
4. Richard Foster, "Crucifying Our Will."

Chapter 9: What's So Glorious About Those Spiritual Riches?

1. Dr. Cliff Welborn, "Supply Line Warfare," Army Logistician, November–December 2008, www.almc.army.mil/alog/issues/NovDec08/spplyline_war.html.

Chapter 10: How Do I Access the Glorious Riches of God?

1. Literally, the title of this post is "A Good Word." You can access it here: www.goingbeyond.com/jewelry-box/a-good-word.

Chapter 12: The Devil Doesn't Want You to Know the Power of Forgiveness

1. "Forgiveness," Wikipedia, http://en.wikipedia.org/wiki/Forgiveness.
2. June Hunt, *Forgiveness: The Freedom to Let Go* (Torrance, CA: Aspire Press, 2013), 10.
3. Oprah on Forgiveness: This Definition Was "Bigger Than an Aha Moment," Huffington Post, March 7, 2013, www.huffingtonpost.com/2013/03/07/oprah-on-forgiveness-how-to-forgive_n_2821736.html.
4. Ronnie Floyd, general editor, *Bible Studies for Life: Students Personal Study Guide* (Nashville: Lifeway Christian Resources, Spring 2015).
5. Ibid.
6. Everett Worthington, *Becoming a More Forgiving Christian: Participant Manual* (Richmond, VA: Virginia Commonwealth University), 9.
7. Ibid., 11.
8. Ibid., 37.

Chapter 13: The Devil Doesn't Want You to Know the Power of the Holy Spirit

1. Andrew Murray, *Waiting on God* (New Kensington, PA: Whitaker House, 1981), 257–258.

Chapter 14: Tear Down the High Places

1. "Your Worthless Gods," Never Thirsty, www.neverthirsty.org/pp/series /REV/REV015/R015.html.

2. Ed Stetzer, "Idolatry Is Alive Today: Why Modern Church Leaders Still Fight an Old Battle," *Christianity Today*, October 8, 2014, www.christianitytoday .com/edstetzer/2014/october/idolatry-is-alive-today-why-modern-church-leaders -still-fig.html.

3. John Piper, "What Is Idolatry?" Desiring God, August 19, 2014, www.desiring god.org/interviews/what-is-idolatry.

4. Jonathan Parnell, "Parenting Means Wrestling Demons," Desiring God, March 4, 2015, www.desiringgod.org/articles/parenting-means-wrestling-demons.

Chapter 15: Train Your Brain to Embrace the Mind of Christ

1. Leighann McCoy, *A Woman's Guide to Hearing God's Voice* (Minneapolis: Bethany House, 2013), 28.

Chapter 18: The Divine Weapon of Praise and Thanksgiving

1. Dr. Caroline Leaf, "C-reactive Protein and How Our Bodies React to Toxic Thought," Dr. Leaf, June 1, 2015, http://drleaf.com/blog/c-reactive-protein -and-how-our-bodies-react-to-toxic-thought.

2. Dr. Pamela Reeve, in Ruth Myers, *31 Days of Praise* (Sisters, OR: Mult-nomah, 1994), 7.

Chapter 19: The Divine Weapon of Intercession

1. Joseph M. Scriven, "What a Friend We Have in Jesus," 1855, public domain.

2. Jeanette Strauss, *From the Courtroom of Heaven to the Throne of Grace and Mercy* (Glorious Creations Publishing, 2011).

3. David Platt, "Relenting Wrath: The Role of Desperate Prayer in the Mystery of Divine Providence," *Together for the Gospel*, http://t4g.org/media/2014/03 /relenting-wrath-the-role-of-desperate-prayer-in-the-mystery-of-divine-providence.

Chapter 27: Loneliness

1. Gary Chapman and Ross Campbell, *The 5 Love Languages of Children* (Chicago: Northfield Publishing, 2012).

Chapter 29: Blended Families

1. Natalie Nichols Gillespie, "Blended Families," Focus on the Family, www .focusonthefamily.com/lifechallenges/relationship-challenges/blended-families /blended-families.

Chapter 33: Substance Abuse and Addictions

1. "Dealing With a Teen Who Struggles With Drug Addiction," Focus on the Family, http://family.custhelp.com/app/answers/detail/a_id/25563/~/dealing -with-a-teen-who-struggles-with-drug-addiction.

Chapter 35: Cancer, Death, and Chronic Illness

1. Tony Snow, "Cancer's Unexpected Blessings," *Christianity Today*, July 20, 2007, www.christianitytoday.com/ct/2007/july/25.30.html.

Leighann McCoy is a sought-after speaker and author of *Spiritual Warfare for Women* and *A Woman's Guide to Hearing God's Voice*. She is the prayer minister at a large Southern Baptist church where her husband serves as pastor. She also leads Never Fail Faith Ministries, a community of believers who connect with one another for encouragement and growth. Visit Leighann online at www.LeighannMcCoy.com, where you can join the community and access prayer and spiritual warfare resources for individuals and churches.

Also From Leighann McCoy

To learn more about Leighann, visit leighannmccoy.com.

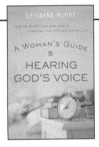

Although God rarely speaks audibly, He is *always* speaking—the hard part is learning how to listen for His still, small voice. Through personal stories and insight into biblical narratives, Leighann McCoy shows you how God speaks and acts amid life's everyday ups and downs.

A Woman's Guide to Hearing God's Voice

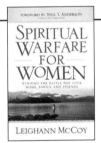

From one woman to another, here is the instruction and assurance you need to protect yourself *and* your loved ones from the harmful ploys of the enemy. Full of invaluable spiritual wisdom and practical tips on identifying the enemy's strategies, overcoming fear, and more, this book will help you find your own path to victory.

Spiritual Warfare for Women